Quick Reference Guide™

Microsoft® Office Professional

Version 4.3

Access 2/Excel 5/PowerPoint 4/Word 6

Gosselin/Schwartz/Toliver/Reidelbach

14 East 38 St New York, NY 10016

First DDC Publishing, Inc. Printing

10 9 8 7 6 5 4 3 2

Catalog No. MO17

ISBN: 1-56243-251-6

Printed in the United States of America

The *DDC Quick Reference Guide for Microsoft Office* saves you hours searching through technical manuals for directions. Step–by–step instructions for essential procedures using mouse and keyboard methods help you get answers fast.

Microsoft Office makes working with applications commonly used in business settings (word processing, spreadsheet, presentation and database) efficient and logical since many commands, menus and dialog boxes are standardized. This powerful program provides an internal visual and procedural consistency while maintaining ultimate flexibility for your individual computing needs. For example, commands for copying, moving, pasting, printing, spell checking, finding and replacing, as well as several other procedures, are the same in **Word, Excel, PowerPoint** and **Access.**

This guide is designed to provides essential commands for the Microsoft Office programs, focusing on universal features and pointing out application–specific essentials. If you want more comprehensive information on any of these programs, please consult the individual DDC Quick Reference Guides for **Word, Excel, PowerPoint** and **Access.**

Authors:

Word	Don Gosselin
Excel	Karl Schwartz
PowerPoint	Pam Toliver
Access	Maria Reidelbach

Editors: Kathy Berkemeyer
                      Rebecca Fiala

Layout: DDC Publishing

INTRODUCTION
TABLE OF CONTENTS
WORD

EXCEL

TABLE OF CONTENTS   iii

POWERPOINT

ACCESS

INDEX...............................327

BASICS

COPY

1. Select information to copy.

2. Click ⬛ .... `Ctrl`+`C`

CUT

1. Select information to cut.

2. Click ✂ .... `Ctrl`+`X`

DELETE

1. Select information to delete.

2. Press **Delete** .... `Del`

DRAG AND DROP

Move

1. Select information to move.

2. Point at selected information and hold mouse button.

   Mouse will change to drag-and-drop pointer

3. Drag to new location; position dotted insertion point where information should appear and release mouse.

Copy

1. Select information to copy.

2. Hold **Ctrl** .... `Ctrl`

3. Point at selected information and hold mouse button.

COPY (CONTINUED)

4. Drag to new location; position dotted insertion point where information should be copied, and release mouse.

NAVIGATE

Go To Command

1. Double-click status bar .... `Ctrl`+`G`

2. Select **Go to What** item .... `Alt`+`W`, `↑` `↓`

3. Select **Enter** text box.............................. `Alt`+`E`

   *NOTE: The name of the **Enter** text box changes depending on the option selected in the **Go to What** list box.*

4. Type number or select name ... *number* or `↑` `↓`

   NOTES: Choices vary depending on selection made in step 2.

   Type + or – before a number to move forward or back.

5. Click [**Next**] [**Previous**] .... `Alt`+`T`/`P`

6. Click [**Close**] to exit .... `Esc`

PASTE

1. Place desired information on clipboard with **Copy** or **Cut** commands

2. Place cursor where information should be pasted.

3. Click 📋.. `Ctrl`+`V`

WORD   3

PRINT

1. Click 🖨 .... `Ctrl`+`P`

2. Select **Print What** drop-down list box .... `Alt`+`P`

3. Select information to print............................ `↑` `↓`

4. Enter number of **Copies** .... `Alt`+`C`,*number*

5. Select **Collate Copies**.............................. `Alt`+`I`
   to sort multiple copies.

6. Choose desired **Page Range** option.

7. Select desired **Print** order .... `Alt`+`R`,`↑` `↓`

8. Select **Print to File** .... `Alt`+`L`
   to print document to a .prn file.

9. Select ⬚ **Options...** ⬚ .... `Alt`+`O`
   for additional print options.

10. Click ⬚ **OK** ⬚ .... `↵`

REDO

The name of the Repeat command changes to display the most recent action (e.g., Repeat Bold, Repeat Copy, etc.)

Repeats the most recent action or allows you to select from a list of recent actions.

Click **redo** ⟳▼ .... `Ctrl`+`Y`

SPIKE

Move Information to Spike

1. Select information to Spike.

2. Press **Ctrl+F3**..............................`Ctrl`+`F3`

3. Repeat steps 1-2 for additional material to Spike.

> *NOTE:*   *You can view the contents of the Spike with the **Edit, AutoText Command**.*

Insert Information from Spike

1. Place cursor where Spike material will appear.

2. Press **Shift+Ctrl+F3**...................`Shift`+`Ctrl`+`F3`

> *NOTE:*   *Selecting this procedure will clear the contents of the Spike. You can also insert information without clearing the Spike by using **AutoText**.*

UNDO

> *NOTE:*   *The name of the **Undo** command will change to display the most recent action (e.g., **Undo Bold**, **Undo Copy**, etc.)*

Click `↶ ▾`...`Ctrl`+`Z`
to reverse most recent action.

WORD

5

MANAGE FILES
CLOSE FILE

Double-click ⬜ .... `Ctrl`+`W`

> *NOTE:* *If the file has not been saved, you will*
> *receive a prompt asking if you want to*
> *save your changes. Selecting **Yes** will save*
> *and close the file if it already has a*
> *filename, or appears the **Save As** dialog*
> *box if it does not.*

CLOSE ALL FILES

1. Hold **Shift** and select **File**............ `Shift`+`Alt`+`F`

2. Select **Close All**...`C`

> *NOTE:* *If a file has not been saved, you will receive*
> *a prompt asking if you want to save your*
> *changes. Selecting **Yes** will save and close*
> *the file if it already has a filename, or will*
> *display the **Save As** dialog box if it does*
> *not.*

FIND FILE
Display Find File Dialog Box

1. Select **File**, **Find File**...................... `Alt`+`F`,`F`

> *NOTE:* *If this is the first time you are using the*
> ***Find File** command, the **Search** dialog box*
> *appears. If you have already used **Find***
> ***File** command, the **Find File** dialog box*
> *appears with the results of your last*
> *search.*

2. Click [**Close**]................................... `Esc`
   to close **Find File** dialog box.

View

—FROM FIND FILE DIALOG BOX—

1. Select **View** drop-down list box............. `Alt`+`V`

2. Select file information to display............... `↑` `↓`

3. Press **Enter**.. `↵`

Search

—FROM FIND FILE DIALOG BOX—

1. Click `Search...` .... `Alt`+`S`

2. Click `Clear` to begin new search .. `Alt`+`C`

3. Select **Location**........... `Alt`+`L`,*drive* or `↑` `↓`

4. Select **File Name** drop-down list box .... `Alt`+`N`

5. Select file type ....`↑` `↓`

6. Select **Rebuild File List** check box........ `Alt`+`R`
   to create new list in **Find File** dialog box
   with new search results.

   *NOTE: If this check box is not selected, the new
   search results will be added to the current
   list.*

7. Select **Include Subdirectories**............... `Alt`+`B`
   check box to search through
   subdirectories, if desired.

8. Click `OK` .... `↵`

*A list of matching files appears in the Listed Files list box of
the Find File dialog box.*

WORD

NEW FILE

Click [🗋] .... `Ctrl`+`N`

A new document is automatically based on NORMAL template.

OPEN FILE

1. Click [📂] .... `Ctrl`+`O`

2. Select **List Files of Type** to open.. `Alt`+`T`, `↑` `↓`

   If you want to be prompted before Word converts file types from other applications:

   Select **Confirm Conversions** check box . `Alt`+`C`

3. Select **Drives** drop-down list box .... `Alt`+`V`

4. Type or select drive letter .... *drive* or `↑` `↓`
   containing the file you want to open.

5. Double-click desired .... `Alt`+`D`, `↑` `↓` `↵`
   directory in **Directories** box containing file to open.

   For help in searching for a particular file:

   Click [**Find File...**] .... `Alt`+`F`

6. Select **Read Only** check box .... `Alt`+`R`
   to prevent changes to document.

7. Double-click file .... `Alt`+`N`, *filename*, `Enter`
   in **File Name** list box.

SAVE FILE

1 Click 🖫 .... Ctrl + S

> *NOTE: If the file you are saving already has a file
> name, the file will be saved and you will be
> returned to your document. If you are
> saving a new, unnamed file, proceed to
> step 2.*

2. Select **Save File as Type** .... Alt + T , ↑ ↓

> *NOTE: The available file types will vary depending
> on choices made during program
> installation.*

3. Select **Dri̲ves** drop-down list box .... Alt + V

4. Type or select drive letter .... *drive* or ↑ ↓
   where you want to store the file.

5. Double-click desired directory in which to store the
   file in **D̲irectories** list box.

6. Select **File N̲ame** list box .... Alt + N

7. Type new file name .... *name*

   To access additional save options:

   Click ⌷ **O̲ptions...** ⌷ .... Alt + O

8. Click ⌷ **OK** ⌷ .... ↵

> *NOTES: Depending on choices selected in **Save
> Options**, the **Summary Info** dialog box
> may be displayed.*

TEMPLATES

*Word uses a special global template, **NORMAL.DOT**. This template can be used like any other template, although it contains global command information such as toolbars, styles, and macros, available to all documents, regardless of the particular template upon which a document is based. Command information contained in other templates, with the exception of styles, can be made available globally with the **File Templates** command.*

Modify Existing Template

1. Complete **Open File** procedure, page 7.
2. Make desired changes to template information/formatting.
3. Save and close file.

DISPLAY OPTIONS

*Word provides many different ways to display and work with documents. In addition to the following choices, various other display options can be selected with the **View** tab under **Tools Options**.*

FULL SCREEN VIEW

Hides all portions of the screen that are not part of the document, such as the menu, toolbars, ruler, and scroll bars.

1. Select **View** menu .... `Alt`+`V`
2. Select **Full Screen**... `U`

   To exit full screen:
   Click .... `Esc`

MASTER DOCUMENT VIEW

*Displays documents in **Master Document** view, used for organizing and maintaining long documents by dividing them into subdocuments. Word automatically assigns a unique file name to subdocuments based on the first characters in the heading that begins a subdocument. You can work with subdocuments just like you would other documents. Subdocuments are enclosed in a box and have a* ***Subdocument*** *icon ▦ next to them.*

Select **View, Master Document** .... `Alt`+`V`,`M`

To switch to Master Document view from Outline:

Click ▦ on **Outlining** toolbar.

NONPRINTING CHARACTERS

Click `¶` .... `Shift`+`Ctrl`+`F8`

VIEWS

Normal View

Click ▤ in lower left of screen................ `Ctrl`+`Alt`+`N`

Outline View

Click ▤ in lower left corner of screen .... `Ctrl`+`Alt`+`O`

*In **Outline view**, paragraphs that do not use heading styles have a hollow square symbol ▱ next to them. These paragraphs are also referred to as **body text**. Paragraphs that use a heading style and are followed by body text have a hollow plus symbol ✛ next to them. Paragraphs that use a heading style but are not followed by any body text have a hollow dash symbol ▱' next to them.*

Page Layout View

Displays documents in Page Layout view, used for showing and working with the actual size, formatting, and layout of information in your document.

Click 🔳 lower left corner of screen.... `Ctrl`+`Alt`+`P`

Print Preview

Click 🔍.. `Ctrl`+`Alt`+`I`

RULER

Toggles display of horizontal and vertical rulers.

> *NOTE: Vertical rulers only appear in Page Layout View or Print Preview.*

Select **View**, **Ruler**........................... `Alt`+`V`, `R`

Zoom

1. Select **View**, **Zoom To** .... `Alt`+`V`, `Z`
2. Choose desired option.

FORMAT/EDIT

AUTOTEXT

Create AutoText

1. Select information you want to use to create an AutoText entry.

> *NOTE: To store paragraph formatting in the AutoText entry, include the paragraph mark along with the selected information.*

2. Click ⌨ .... `Alt`+`E`, `X`
3. Select **Name** text box .... `Alt`+`N`

CREATE AUTOTEXT (CONTINUED)

4. Type name for AutoText entry .... *name*
   (up to 32 characters, including spaces).

5. Select **Make AutoText Entry** .... [Alt]+[M]
   Available To drop–down list box.

6. Select where to make entry available .... [↑][↓]
   (default is **All Documents** [normal.dot])

7. Click [**Add**] .... [Alt]+[A]

Edit AutoText Command

Inserts AutoText entries using the Edit, AutoText command.

1. Place cursor in document where AutoText entry
   should be placed.

2. Click 🖱 .... [Alt]+[E], [X]

3. Choose how AutoText entry will be inserted into
   document.

4. Double–click AutoText entry.

Insert AutoText

> NOTE: This procedure will automatically insert
> AutoText entries as formatted text. To
> insert AutoText entries as unformatted
> text, use the **Edit** AutoText command,
> above.

1. Place cursor in document where you want to insert
   an AutoText entry.

2. Type name of existing AutoText entry............ *name*
   (or the first few letters that identify an entry).

3. Click 🖱 .... [F3]

WORD

Edit AutoText

1. Insert AutoText entry to edit *(see above)*.

2. Make desired changes.

3. Select information that comprising AutoText entry.

4. Click 🖳 .... Alt + E , X

5. Select **Name** text box .... Alt + N

6. Type or select name .... *name* or ↑ ↓
   of AutoText entry you are editing.

7. Click [**Add**] .... Alt + A

8. Click [**Yes**] .... Alt + Y
   when confirmation dialog box appears.

Delete AutoText

1. Click 🖳 .... Alt + E , X

2. Select **Name** text box .... Alt + N

3. Type or select name .... *name* or ↑ ↓
   of AutoText entry to delete.

4. Click [**Delete**] .... Alt + D

5. Click [**Cancel**] .... Esc

BORDERS AND SHADING

Format Borders and Shade Borders

1 Select desired information to which you want to
   add border.

14 WORD

FORMAT BORDERS AND SHADE BORDERS (CONTINUED)

2. Select **Format, Borders and Shading**... `Alt`+`O`, `B`

3. Select [**B**ulleted] .... `Alt`+`B`

4. Choose desired border style from **Presets**.

5. Select desired **Color** .... `Alt`+`C`, `↑` `↓`

    To remove specific border:

    a. Select **Bo_r_der** model........................ `Alt`+`R`

    b. Select side to remove border . `↑` `↓` `←` `→`

    c. Select **N_o_ne**..................................... `Alt`+`O`

6. Select **From Text** scroll box................... `Alt`+`F`

7. Enter amount of space between borders and text.

8. Click [**OK**] .... `↵`

Shading

1. Select information to shade.

2. Select **Format, Borders and Shading**.. `Alt`+`O`, `B`

3. Select [Shading] .... `Alt`+`S`

    *NOTE: The **Shading** tab is not available if a
    graphic was selected in step 1.*

4. Select **Sha_d_ing** pattern .... `Alt`+`D`, `↑` `↓`

5. Select **Foreground** color .... `Alt`+`F`, `↑` `↓`

6. Select **B_a_ckground** color.......... `Alt`+`A`, `↑` `↓`

7. Click [**OK**] .... `↵`

BULLETS AND NUMBERING

Add/Remove Bullet List

1. Select information for which you want to add or remove bullets.

2. Select **Format, Bullets & Numbering**.... `Alt`+`O`,`N`

3. Select [**Bulleted**] .... `Alt`+`B`

4. Press **Tab** to reach bullet format list .... `Tab`

5. Select bullet format .... `↑` `↓` `←` `→`

   If you do not want selected information formatted with hanging indent.

   Deselect **Hanging Indent** text box .... `Alt`+`A`

   To remove bullets from selected information:

   Click [**Remove**] .... `Alt`+`R`

   NOTES: *This option is unavailable if selected information is not formatted with bullets or numbers.*

   *The **Remove** button removes all bullet and numbering options selected from any of the available tabs in the **Bullets and Numbering** dialog box.*

6. Click [**OK**] to apply bullet format...... `↵`.

Add/Remove Numbered List

1. Select information for which you want to add/remove numbers.

2. Select **Format, Bullets & Numbering**... `Alt`+`O`,`N`

ADD/REMOVE NUMBERED LIST (CONTINUED)

3. Selected ⎰ Nᵤmbered ⎱ .... **Alt**+**N**

4. Press **Tab** to reach number format list .... **Tab**

5. Select number format .... **↑** **↓** **←** **→**

If you do not want selected information to be formatted with hanging indent:

Deselect **Hanging Indent** text box .... **Alt**+**A**

To remove numbers from the selected information:

Click ⎰ **Remove** ⎱ .... **Alt**+**R**

NOTES: This option is unavailable if selected information is not formatted with bullets or numbers.

*The **Remove** button will remove all bullet and numbering options selected from any of the available tabs in the **Bullets and Numbering** dialog box.*

6. Click ⎰ **OK** ⎱ to apply number format .. **↵**

CHARACTER FORMAT

Format Font

1. Select text to change.

2. Select **Format, Font** .... **Ctrl**+**D**

3. Select ⎰ Font ⎱ ...... **Alt**+**N**

4. Select desired **Font** .... **Alt**+**F**, *font* or **↑** **↓**

WORD

17

FORMAT FONT (CONTINUED)

5. Select desired **Font Style** .... `Alt`+`O`, `↑` `↓`

   NOTE: Choices vary with selected font.

6. Select desired **Size** .... `Alt`+`S`, *size* or `↑` `↓`

7. Select desired **Underline** .... `Alt`+`U`, `↑` `↓`

8. Select desired **Color** .... `Alt`+`C`, `↑` `↓`

9. Choose desired **Effects** option(s).

   *NOTE: To set custom superscript and subscript positions, see **Character Spacing**, below.*

   To use selected options as default settings for current document and all new documents based on it:

   a. Click `Default...` .... `Alt`+`D`

   b. Click `Yes` .... `Alt`+`Y`
      when confirmation dialog box appears.

   *NOTE: Selecting the **Default** button sets the defaults for options selected in the **Font** tab as well as the **Character Spacing** tab.*

10. Click `OK` .... `↵`

Character Spacing

—FROM FONT DIALOG BOX—

1. Select **Character Spacing** tab .... `Alt`+`R`

2. Select **Spacing** option .... `Alt`+`S`, `↑` `↓`

3. Select **By** text box.................................. `Alt`+`B`

CHARACTER SPACING (CONTINUED)

4. Type number for desired spacing .... *number*

5. Select **P**osition option .... `Alt`+`P`, `↑` `↓`

6. Select **B**y text box .... `Alt`+`Y`

7. Type number for desired spacing .... *number*

8. Select **Kerning for Fonts** check box....... `Alt`+`K`

9. Select **P**oints and Above text box.......... `Alt`+`O`

10. Type number for point size .... *number*
    at which Word automatically adjusts kerning.

    *NOTES: To use selected options as default settings
    for current document and all new
    documents based on it, see procedure
    above.*

    *Selecting the **Default** button sets the
    defaults for options selected in the
    Character Spacing tab as well as the **Font**
    tab.*

11. Click [**OK**   ] .... `↵`

Character Format Keyboard Shortcuts

FORMAT:	PRESS:
All capital letters	Shift + Ctrl + A
Bold	Ctrl + B
Create Symbol font	Shift + Ctrl + Q
Display nonprinting characters	Shift + Ctrl + *
Font box (Formatting toolbar)	Shift + Ctrl + F
Hidden text	Shift + Ctrl + H
Italicize	Ctrl + I
Letters–toggle case	Shift + F3
Point size box (Formatting toolbar)	Shift + Ctrl + P
Point size–decrease/increase 1 point	Ctrl + [/]
Point size–decrease/decrease to next available point size.	Shift + Ctrl + < / >
Remove formatting	Shift + Ctrl + Z
Small capital letters	Shift + Ctrl + K
Subscript	Ctrl + =
Superscript	Shift + Ctrl + =
Underline–single	Ctrl + U
Underline–double	Shift + Ctrl + D
Underline–word only	Shift + Ctrl + W

Drop Cap

1. Select letter/text to format as dropped cap.

2. Select **Format**, **Drop Cap** .... Alt + O , D

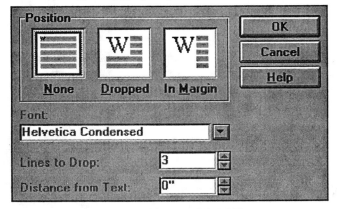

DROP CAP DIALOG BOX

3. Choose desired dropped cap position option.

4. Select **Font** .... Alt + F ,*font* or ↑ ↓

   NOTE: *This option is unavailable if **None** was selected in previous step.*

5. Select **Lines to Drop** .... Alt + L ,*number* to extend dropped cap downward.

   NOTE: *This option is unavailable if **None** was selected above.*

6. Enter **Distance from Text** .... Alt + X ,*number* between dropped cap and body of paragraph.

7. Click 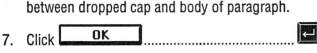 .... ⏎

Symbols

1. Place cursor in document in which to insert character.

2. Select **I**nsert, **S**ymbol .... `Alt`+`I`, `S`

3. Select 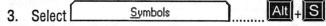 Symbols .... `Alt`+`S`

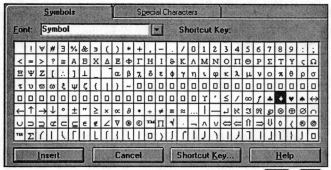

4. Select **F**ont drop–down list box .... `Alt`+`F`

5. Select font containing character .... `↑` `↓`

6. Double–click desired character.

   To assign selected character to a shortcut key:

   Click [**Shortcut Key...**] .... `Alt`+`K`

Special Characters

1. Place cursor where you wish to insert character.

2. Select **Insert**, **Symbol** .... `Alt` + `I`, `S`

4. Select [S<u>p</u>ecial Characters   ] .... `Alt` + `P`

5. Select desired **Character** .... `Alt` + `C`, `↑` `↓`

   To assign new shortcut key to selected character:
   Click [**Shortcut Key...**] .... `Alt` + `K`

6. Click [**Insert**   ] .... `Alt` + `I`

Insert Special Characters with Keyboard

SPECIAL CHARACTER:	PRESS:
Column break	`Shift` + `Ctrl` + `Enter`
Copyright symbol	`Alt` + `Ctrl` + `C`
Ellipsis	`Alt` + `Ctrl` + `.`
Line break	`Shift` + `Enter`
Nonbreaking hyphen	`Shift` + `Ctrl` + `-`
Nonbreaking space..................	`Shift` + `Ctrl` + `Space`
Optional hyphen	`Ctrl` + `-`
Page break	`Ctrl` + `Enter`
Registered trademark ® symbol	`Ctrl` + `Alt` + `R`
Trademark ™ symbol	`Ctrl` + `Alt` + `T`

Copy Character Formats

After applying desired character formats, they can be easily copied to other text in the document.

> *NOTE:* *When using the following procedures, Word will copy the character style along with the applied character formatting for the first character in a selection. If a paragraph mark is selected, Word will also copy the paragraph style in addition to the character style and applied character formatting for the first character in the selection.*

Format Painter

1. Select information containing format to copy.

2. Click ![brush icon] to copy formatting to a single location.

The mouse pointer changes to a ![brush pointer icon]

3. Position mouse pointer over information to which you want to copy character formatting.

4. Hold mouse button.

5. Drag to select information to which you want to copy character formatting.

6. Release mouse button.

   If you double–clicked Format Painter in step 2:

   a. Repeat steps 3–6 to copy character formatting to additional locations.

   b. Press **Esc** to turn off .... Esc

FIELDS

Fields are used to retrieve and display information in a document from a variety of different sources.

Insert Field Command

1. Place cursor in document in which to insert field.

2. Select **Insert, Field** .... `Alt` + `I` , `E`

3. Select desired field **Categories** ..... `Alt` + `C` , `↑` `↓`

4. Select **Field Name** .... `Alt` + `N` , `↑` `↓`

   To choose specific options for selected field:

   Click `Options...` .... `Alt` + `O`

   *NOTES: This option is not available if **Numbering** was selected in step 3.*

   *The **Field Options** dialog box appears for the selected field. Press **F1** for on–line Help with specific fields, or see your Word documentation for more information.*

   *You can also select the **Field Codes** text box and type specific field instructions after the name of the selected field.*

5. Select **Preserve Formatting** .... `Alt` + `P`
   During Updates check box, if desired.

   *NOTE: This option is enabled by default and is not available if **Numbering** was selected in step 5.*

6. Click `OK` .... `↵`

FIND AND REPLACE

Find

*NOTE: To repeat the last search, press **Shift+F4**.*

1. Place cursor at position in document where you want to begin search.

2. Press **Ctrl+F** .... `Ctrl`+`F`

3. Select **Find What** text box .... `Alt`+`N`

4. Type text.. `↑` `↓`

    To search for special characters:

    a. Click `Special ▼` .... `Alt`+`E`

    b. Choose desired special characters........... *letter*

5. Click `Format ▼` .... `Alt`+`O`

6. Choose desired format for which to search.

    To clear all formatting from Find dialog box:

    Click `No Formatting` .... `Alt`+`T`

    *NOTE: You can search for specific formatting without entering any text into the **Find What** text box in step 4.*

7. Select direction...................... `Alt`+`S`, `↑` `↓`

8. Choose additional search check box options.

9. Click `Find Next` .... `Alt`+`F`

    To open Replace dialog box:

    Click `Replace...` .... `Alt`+`R`

Replace

1. Place cursor in document to search.
2. Press **Ctrl+H** .... `Ctrl`+`H`
3. Select **Find What** text box.................. `Alt`+`N`
4. Repeat steps 4–7 under **Find**, above.
5. Select **Replace With** text box .... `Alt`+`P`
6. Repeat steps 4–7 under **Find**, above.
7. Click desired **Replace** option(s).
8. Click `Cancel` to close........................ `Esc`

FRAMES

In order to view, resize, or reposition a frame, it is necessary to be in Page Layout view or Print Preview.

Insert Frame

NOTES: If you are inserting a frame in Normal view, you will receive a prompt asking if you want to switch to Page Layout view.

You cannot insert a frame from Outline view or Master Document view.

Frame Selected Information

1. Select information around which you want to place frame.
2. Click ▦ on **Forms/Drawing** toolbar ... `Alt`+`I`, `F`

Insert Empty Frame

1. Place cursor in document in which to insert frame.

   NOTE: Make sure no information is selected.

2. Click 🗔 on **Forms/Drawing** toolbar... `Alt`+`I`, `F`

The mouse pointer will change to a crosshair +.

3. Position mouse at upper left corner of where you want frame to appear on page.

4. Hold mouse button.

5. Drag mouse until frame reaches desired size.

6. Release mouse button.

Format Frame

1. Select frame.

2. Select **F**o**rmat**, **Fra**m**e** .... `Alt`+`O`, `M`

3. Choose desired frame options.

4. Click ` OK ` .... `↵`

INSERT DATE AND TIME

1. Place cursor in document where you want to insert current date or time.

2. Select **I**nsert, **Date and **T**ime .... `Alt`+`I`, `T`

3. Select date or time format......................... `↑` `↓`
   from **Available Formats** list box.

   To insert selected format as a field:

   Select **I**nsert as Field check box............ `Alt`+`I`

4. Click ` OK ` .... `↵`

PAGE AND SECTION SETUP

1. Place cursor in document where you want to change margin settings, or select desired information whose margins you want to change.

2. Double–click blank area .... [Alt]+[F], [U] of horizontal or vertical ruler.

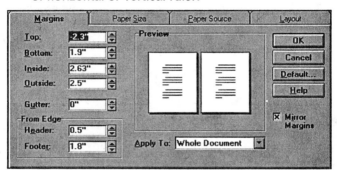

3. Select desired options.

4. Click [OK] .... [↵]

Newspaper–Style Columns

1. Place cursor in document where you want to change the number of newspaper–style columns, or select desired information for which you want to change the number of newspaper–style columns.

2. Select **Format**, **Columns** .... [Alt]+[O], [C]

3. Select desired column options.

   OR

   a. Place cursor in document in which to apply newspaper–style columns, or select desired information.

NEWSPAPER-STYLE COLUMNS (CONTINUED)

NOTE: *Newspaper–style columns are section*
specific. Section breaks will be inserted
above and below any selected information.

b. Click 🔲 on standard toolbar.

c. Hold mouse button, drag over sizing grid to
select desired number of columns and release
mouse.

Headers/Footers

Select <u>V</u>iew, <u>H</u>eader and Footer........... **Alt**+**V**, **H**

The header and footer areas appear, enclosed by a nonprinting
dashed line, along with the **Header and Footer** *toolbar.*

Insert Page Numbers Command

1. Select <u>I</u>nsert, Page N<u>u</u>mbers .... **Alt**+**I**, **U**

2. Select desired options.

3. Click **OK** to close .... ↵

Insert Break

1. Position cursor where you want to insert a new
break.

2. Select <u>I</u>nsert, <u>B</u>reak...................... **Alt**+**I**, **B**

3. Choose desired break option.

4. Click **OK** .... ↵

PARAGRAPH FORMAT

Indents and Spacing

1. Place cursor in paragraph to format, or select multiple paragraphs.

2. Select **F**ormat, **P**aragraph .... Alt +O, P

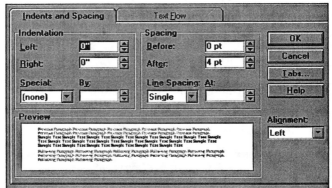

3. Select **Indents and Spacing** options.

4. Click **OK** when finished .... ↵

Text Flow

1. Place cursor in paragraph to format, or select multiple paragraphs.

2. Select **Format**, **Paragraph**............ `Alt`+`O`, `P`

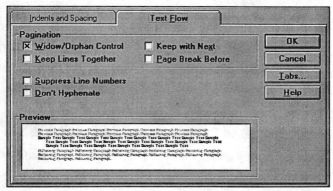

3. Select [Text Flow] .... `Alt`+`F`

5. Choose desired options.

6. Click [OK] .... `⏎`

STYLES

Apply Style

1. Select paragraphs to which you want to apply paragraph style, or select characters to which you want to apply character style.

2. Select **Format**, **Style** .... `Alt`+`O`, `S`

3. Select desired **List** style .... `Alt`+`L`, `↑` `↓`

4. Select desired **Styles**.............. `Alt`+`S`, `↑` `↓`

   NOTE: Paragraph style names are bold, character styles are not.

5. Click [Apply] .... `Alt`+`A`

Create Style

1. Select **Format, Style**...................... `Alt`+`O`,`S`

2. Click [**New...**] .... `Alt`+`N`

3. Enter new style **Name**..................`Alt`+`N`,*text*
   (up to 253 characters).

4. Select desired **Style Type** .... `Alt`+`T`, `↑``↓`

5. Select **Based On** style............. `Alt`+`B`, `↑``↓`

   NOTE: By default, new paragraph styles are based on the style applied to the active paragraph.

6. Select desired **Style**............... `Alt`+`S`, `↑``↓`
   for Following Paragraph.

   *NOTE: This option is not available if **Character** was selected for **Style Type** in step 7.*

7. Click [**Format ▼**] .... `Alt`+`O`

8. Choose desired format option for new style.

9. Click [**Shortcut Key...**] .... `Alt`+`K`
   to assign the new style to a key combination.

The Customize dialog box, opened to the Keyboard tab, appears.

   NOTE: In addition to shortcut keys, styles can also be assigned to toolbars. See your Word documentation or on–line Help for more information.

CREATE STYLE (CONTINUED)

10. Select **Add to Template** check box......... `Alt`+`A`
    to add new style to current document template.

11. Click `OK` .... `↵`
    to create new style and close **New Style** dialog box.

12. Click `Close` .... `Esc`

Delete Style

> *NOTE: Built-in styles, such as heading level styles, cannot be deleted.*

1. Select **Format**, **Style** menu............. `Alt`+`O`, `S`

2. Select **List** drop-down list box.............. `Alt`+`L`

3. Select desired style option .... `↑` `↓`

4. Select desired **Styles**............... `Alt`+`S`, `↑` `↓`

> *NOTE: Paragraph style names are bold, character styles are not.*

5. Click `Delete` .... `Alt`+`D`

6. Click `Yes` .... `↵`
    when **Delete Confirmation** dialog box appears.

7. Click `Close` .... `Esc`

Style Gallery

Copies all styles from a different template to the current document. Displays different previews of the available template styles including a preview of what the document will look like when the new styles have been applied.

STYLE GALLERY (CONTINUED)

> *NOTE:*   *Copying styles from the **Style Gallery**
> automatically overwrites styles in the
> document with the same style name.*

1. Select F**o**rmat, **Style Gallery** .... Alt + O , G

2. Select desired **T**emplate .... Alt + T , ↑ ↓
   containing styles to copy.

3. Choose desired **Preview** option.

4. Click [**OK**   ] .... ↵
   to close **Style Gallery** dialog box
   and apply styles from selected template.

AUTOFORMAT

> *NOTE:*   *This command does not format tables. To
> format tables automatically, use the **Table
> AutoFormat** command.*

Allows you to review formatting changes.

1. Place cursor in document to format, or select
   desired information.

WORD

2. Select **Format, AutoFormat**.......... `Alt`+`O`, `A`

A prompt appears telling you Word is about to format the document or selected information.

3. Click `[ OK ]` .... `↵`

> *NOTE:*   *Word automatically formats the document with styles from the attached template, then display the* **AutoFormat** *dialog box.*

4. Click `[Accept]` or `[Reject All]` .. `Alt`+`A`/`R`

To review individual style changes:

a. Click `[Review Changes...]` .... `Alt`+`C`

b. Choose desired command.

c. Click `[ Close ]` .... `Esc`
to exit **Review AutoFormat Changes**

To choose styles from different template:

Click `[ Style Gallery... ]` .... `Alt`+`S`

TABS

Set/Change Tab Stop

1. Select paragraphs for which you want to format tab stops.

2. Double–click existing tab.............. `Alt`+`O`, `T`
in horizontal ruler.

3. Enter **Tab Stop Position**............`Alt`+`T`,*number*

4. Choose desired **Alignment** option.

SET/CHANGE TAB STOP (CONTINUED)

5. Choose **Leader** options:

6. Click [<u>S</u>et] .... [Alt]+[S]

7. Repeat steps 3–6 to set additional tab stops.

8. Click [OK] .... [↵]

Remove Individual Tab Stop(s)

1. Select paragraphs for which you want to remove tab stop(s).

2. Select **F**o**rmat**, **T**abs .... [Alt]+[O], [T]

3. Select **T**ab **Stop Position** .... [Alt]+[T], [↑][↓]

4. Click [Cl**e**ar] .... [Alt]+[E]

5. Repeat steps 3–4 to remove additional tab stops.

6. Click [OK] .... [↵]

Remove All Tab Stops

1. Select paragraphs for which you want to remove tab stops.

2. Select **F**o**rmat**, **T**abs .... [Alt]+[O], [T]

3. Click [Clear **A**ll] .... [Alt]+[A]

4. Click [OK] .... [↵]

Default Tab Stops

> NOTE: Default tab stops cannot be set for individual paragraphs, only for an entire document.

1. Select **Format, Tabs** .... `Alt`+`O`, `T`

2. Enter **Default Tab Stops** .... `Alt`+`F`, *number*

3. Click `OK` .... `↵`

Set Tab Stops on the Ruler

> NOTE: In order to set tab leaders or change default tab stops, it is necessary to use the **Format, Tabs** command (see above).

1. Select paragraphs in which to set tab stops.

2. Click **Tab Alignment** button at far left of horizontal ruler until desired tab stop button is visible:

`L`	`⊥`	`⌐`	`⊥·`
Left–aligned	Center	Right–aligned	Decimal

3. Point mouse at desired tab stop position in horizontal ruler.

4. Click mouse button to set tab.

5. Repeat steps 2–4 to set additional tab stops for selected paragraphs.

Remove Tab Stops

1. Select paragraphs from which to remove tab stops.

2. Position mouse over tab stop to remove in horizontal ruler.

3. Hold mouse button; drag tab off ruler. Release mouse button.

TABLES

CELL HEIGHT AND WIDTH

1. Select column/cell, or group of columns/cells to change.

2. Double–click column marker .... Alt + A , W in horizontal ruler.

3. Select **C**olumn tab .... Alt + C

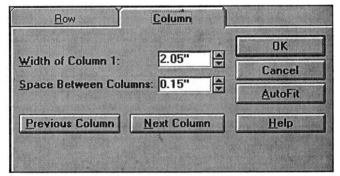

4. Choose desired width/space options.

5. Click [OK] .... ↵

CONVERT TABLE TO TEXT

1. Select table or rows within table to convert to paragraphs.

2. Select **Ta**ble, **Con**v**ert Table to Text** Alt + A , V

3. Choose desired column separator option.

4. Click [OK] .... ↵

CONVERT TEXT TO TABLES

NOTE: *In addition to the following steps, you can also quickly convert text to tables by selecting the desired information and clicking the **Insert Table** button on the standard toolbar, or by selecting **Table**, **Insert Table**. Word automatically decides where to insert columns and rows into the selected text.*

1. Select paragraphs to convert to table.

2. Select **Table, Convert Text to Table** `Alt`+`A`, `V`

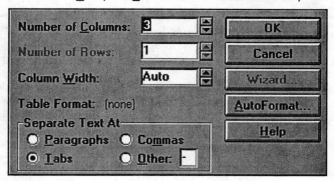

3. Select desired options.

4. Click **OK** .... `⏎`

DELETE CELLS

1. Select cell/group of cells to delete.

2. Select **Table, Delete Cells** .... `Alt`+`A`, `D`

3. Choose desired delete cells option.

4. Click **OK** .... `⏎`

DELETE ROWS/COLUMNS

1. Select row/group of rows, or column/group of columns to delete.

2. Click ✂ .... Ctrl + X

DISPLAY GRIDLINES

Select **Table, Gridlines** .... Alt + A , L

INSERT CELLS

1. Select cell/group of cells.

   NOTE: The number of selected cells is the number of new cells added.

2. Click ▦ .... Alt + A , I

3. Choose desired new cells insertion option.

4. Click [OK] .... ↵

INSERT ROWS

1. Select row/group of rows.

   NOTE: The number of selected rows is the number of new rows added.

2. Click ▦ .... Alt + A , I

INSERT COLUMNS

1. Select a column or group of columns.

   NOTE: The number of selected column will be the number of new column added.

New columns are inserted to the left of the selected columns.

2. Click ▦ .... Alt + A , I

INSERT TABLE

Inserts a table using the Table, Insert Table command, allowing you to specify column widths and apply AutoFormats. This command also allows you to select the Table Wizard.

1. Place cursor where table is to appear.
2. Select **Table, Insert Table**............. [Alt]+[A], [I]
3. Choose desired options.
4. Click [OK] .... [↵]

MERGE CELLS

1. Select cells to merge.
2. Select **Table, Merge Cells** .... [Alt]+[A], [M]

NAVIGATE IN TABLE

Next cell .... [Tab]

Previous cell .... [Shift]+[Tab]

Right/left one character .... [→][←]

One row up/down .... [↑][↓]

First/last cell in current row .... [Alt]+[Home] or [End]

First/last cell in current column .... [Alt]+[Page Up] or [Page Down]

SORT

1. Select information (table rows/paragraphs) to sort.
2. Select **Table, Sort**........................... [Alt]+[A], [T]

> *NOTE:* *The name of the **Sort** command changes between **Sort** if table rows are selected, or **Sort Text** if paragraphs are selected.*

SORT (CONTINUED)

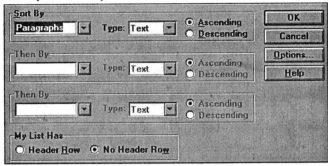

3. Choose sort options.

4. Click **OK** to begin sort........................ ⏎

SPLIT CELLS

1. Select cell/group of cells to split.

2. Select **Table, Split Cells**................. Alt + A , P

3. Type number .... *number*
   in **Number of Columns** text box.

   > NOTE: Each selected cell is split into the number
   > of cells selected in the **Number of Columns**
   > text box.

4. Click **OK** .... ⏎

SPLIT TABLE

1. Place cursor in row in which table is to appear.

2. Press **Shift+Ctrl+Enter** .... Shift + Ctrl + Enter

   > NOTE: Delete the paragraph mark between two
   > tables to remove a split.

TABLE AUTOFORMAT

1. Place cursor in table in which to apply automatic format.

2. Select **Table, Table AutoFormat** .... [Alt]+[A],[F]

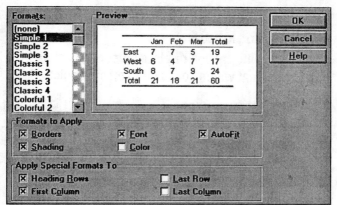

3. Select desired **Formats** .... [Alt]+[T], [↑][↓]

4. Choose desired **Formats to Apply** option.

5. Choose desired **Apply Special Formats To** option.

6. Click [OK   ] .... [↵]

TABS IN CELLS

1. Place cursor where tab character is to appear.

2. Press **Ctrl+Tab** .... [Ctrl]+[Tab]

   *NOTE: Word automatically aligns numbers and other information contained in a cell if it is formatted with a single **decimal tab** (but not other types of tabs). Therefore, it is not necessary to insert a tab character if a single decimal tab is set in a cell.*

REFERENCES
BOOKMARKS

Bookmbarks are used for marking the location of information in a document. Bookmarks are also used in cross–references and for generating a range of pages for an index entry.

Define Bookmark

1. Select information or place cursor at location in document where you want to create bookmark.

2. Press **Shift+Ctrl+F5**.................. `Shift`+`Ctrl`+`F5`

3. Type **Bookmark Name**................ `Alt`+`B`,*name* (up to 40 characters—cannot include spaces).

   OR

   Type or select bookmark name....*name* of `↑``↓` to redefine existing bookmark.

4. Click `Add` .... `Alt`+`A`

Go To Bookmark

NOTE: You can also jump to a bookmark using the Go To command.

1. Press **Shift+Ctrl+F5**.................. `Shift`+`Ctrl`+`F5`

2. Double–click .... `Alt`+`B`,`↑``↓`,`Alt`+`G` bookmark to which you want to move.

3. Click `Close` .... `Esc`

CAPTIONS

Insert Caption
1. Select item for which you want to add a caption.
2. Select **Insert, Caption** .... `Alt`+`I`, `I`
3. Choose desired options.
4. Click ` OK ` .... `↵`

CROSS–REFERENCES

Cross–references in Word, created with REF fields, can refer to footnotes, endnotes, bookmarks, captions, or paragraphs created using heading styles.

1. Place cursor in document where you want to insert a cross–reference.
2. Select **Insert, Cross–reference** ...... `Alt`+`I`, `R`

   NOTE: *The choices in the **Cross–reference** dialog box will vary depending on the available references items in the active document.*

3. Choose desired options.
4. Click ` Insert ` .... `Alt`+`I`

FOOTNOTES/ENDNOTES

Insert Footnote
1. Place cursor in document where you want to insert a footnote or endnote.
2. Select **Insert, Footnote** .... `Alt`+`I`, `N`
3. Choose desired note type options.
4. Choose desired **Numbering** option.

INSERT FOOTNOTE (CONTINUED)

To insert special character:

Click [**Symbol...**] .... [Alt]+[S]

5. Click [**OK**] .... [↵]

6. Type text for footnote or endnote .... *text*.

7. Click [**Close**] .... [Shift]+[Alt]+[C]

Display/Edit Footnote or Endnote

*NOTE: You can also jump to a footnote or endnote using the **Go To** command.*

1. Double–click footnote/endnote ...... [Alt]+[V], [F]
   mark in document.

2. Select **Notes** box .... [Shift]+[Alt]+[N]

3. Choose note type option to display.

   *NOTE: Both choices, **All Footnotes** or **All Endnotes** are only available if a footnote or an endnote, respectively, has already been inserted into the document.*

4. Make desired changes to footnotes or endnotes.

5. Click [**Close**] .... [Shift]+[Alt]+[C]
   to close **Note** pane.

Delete Footnote/Endnote

1. Select footnote or endnote mark in document representing the footnote or endnote you want to delete.

2. Press **Delete** .... [Del]

INDEX AND TABLES

Mark Index Entry

1. Select information you want to use as index entry or position cursor in document where you want to insert index entry.

2. Press **Shift+Alt+X** .... Shift + Alt + X

3. Type **Main Entry** text .... Alt + E , *text*

4. Type **Subentry** text .... Alt + S , *text*

5. Choose desired **Page Number Format** option.

6. Click [**Mark Entry...**] .... Alt + M
   to mark single occurrence of index entry.

   OR

   Click [**Mark All**] .... Alt + A
   to mark all occurrences of index entry in document.

   *NOTE: The **Mark All** button is only available if text was selected in step 1.*

7. Repeat steps 2-6 to insert additional entries.

8. Click [**Close**] .... Esc

Concordance File

Creates a concordance file, used for automatically marking index entries in a document with AutoMark (see below).

1. Create new file.

2. Insert two–column table.

3. In first column of table, type text you want Word to search for when creating index entries.

4. In second column of table, type index entries exactly as you want them to appear in index.

> *NOTES: Entries in both columns of the table are case–sensitive. Create a new row for each index reference and entry.*
>
> *Instead of a table, concordance file entries can also be separated by tabs.*

5. Save file.

AutoMark

Creates index entries in the current document, from index entries contained in a concordance file (see above).

1. Select **Insert, Index and Tables**...... Alt + I , X

2. Select [Index] .... Alt + X

3. Click [AutoMark...] .... Alt + U

4. Select **List Files of Type** list box .... Alt + T

5. Select concordance file type .... ↑ ↓

6. Select **Drives** .... Alt + V ,*drive or* ↑ ↓ containing concordance file.

WORD   49

AUTOMARK (CONTINUED)

7. Double–click directory in **Directories** list box that contains concordance file.

8. Double–click concordance file in **File Name** list box.

Compile Index

1. Place cursor in document where you want to insert index.

2. Select **Insert**, **Index and Tables** ..... `Alt`+`I`, `X`

3. Select [Index   ] .... `Alt`+`X`

4. Choose desired index **Type** option.

5. Select desired index **Formats** ... `Alt`+`T`, `↑` `↓`

   To create custom index format:

   a. Select **Formats**, **Custom Style** `Alt`+`T`, `↑` `↓`

   b. Click [**Modify...**] .... `Alt`+`M`

   *NOTE: This option is only available if **Custom Style** was selected in previous step.*

6. Select **Right Align Page Numbers** .... `Alt`+`R`

   *NOTE: This option is unavailable if **Run–in** was selected in step 4.*

7. Type number of **Columns** .... `Alt`+`O`, *number*

8. Select **Tab Leader** .... `Alt`+`B`, `↑` `↓`

   *NOTE: This option is unavailable if **Run–in** was selected in step 4.*

9. Click [**OK**] .... `↵`

TABLE OF CONTENTS

Mark Table of Contents Entry

Creates table entries for compilation into a table of contents.

1. Select information to use as table entry, or position cursor in where you want to insert table entry.

2. Press **Shift+Alt+O** .... `Shift`+`Alt`+`O`

3. Type **Entry** text .... `Alt`+`E`, *text*

   NOTE: *Any text selected in step 1 will appear in the **Entry** text box.*

4. Select **Table Identifier** .... `Alt`+`I`, `↑``↓`

5. Select desired **Level** .... `Alt`+`L`, *number*

6. Click `Mark` .... `Alt`+`M`

Compile Table of Contents

Compiles a table of contents in the current document. By default, Word compiles a table of contents from heading styles, although you can also use other styles and table entry fields.

1. Place cursor where table of contents is to appear.

2. Select **Insert, Index and Tables** ...... `Alt`+`I`, `X`

3. Select `Table of Contents` .... `Alt`+`C`

4. Select desired **Format** .... `Alt`+`T`, `↑``↓`

   To create custom table of contents format:

   a. Select **Formats, Custom Style** .. `Alt`+`T`, `↑``↓`

COMPILE TABLE OF CONTENTS (CONTINUED)

b. Click | **Modify...** | .... `Alt`+`M`

*NOTE: This option is only available if **Custom**
         Style was selected in previous step.*

5. Choose desired page number option.

6. Select **Show Levels**.................... `Alt`+`L`,*number*

7. Select **Tab Leader**.................... `Alt`+`B`,`↑``↓`

**To create table of contents with styles other than
heading styles, or to include table entry fields:**

a. Click | **Options...** | .... `Alt`+`O`

b. Select **TOC Level** list box................. `Alt`+`L`

c. Select style .... `↑``↓`

d. Type number for level. ....*number*

*NOTE: Styles that have been selected to use for
         compiling the table of contents will have a
         check mark next to them.*

e. Select **Table Entry Fields** .... `Alt`+`E`
    to include table entry fields
    when compiling table of contents.

f. Deselect **Styles** check box .... `Alt`+`S`
    to use only table entry fields
    when compiling table of contents.

**To restore Table of Contents dialog box
settings to use heading styles:**

Click | **Reset** | .... `Alt`+`R`

COMPILE TABLE OF CONTENTS (CONTINUED)

g. Click [OK] .... ↵
to close **Table of Contents** dialog box.

8. Click [OK] .... ↵
to compile table of contents.

TABLE OF AUTHORITIES

*Tables of Authorities are created using two types of citations: long citations and short ones. **Long citations**, in a legal document, are used only once and contain the entire text of the citation. Any further reference to the same source is called a **short citation** and contains a brief summary of the text contained in the associated long citation. Long citations must appear first in a document.*

Citations are created using TA fields. To edit the text of a citation, it is necessary to edit the hidden text contained in the field codes.

Mark Citation

1. Select information you want to use as a long citation, or position cursor where you want to insert a citation entry.

2. Press **Shift+Alt+I** .... Shift + Alt + I

3. Select **Selected Text** text box .... Alt + T

4. Create or edit text for long citation.

5. Select citation **Category** .... Alt + C , ↑ ↓

6. Create or edit **Short Citation** .... Alt + S ,*text*

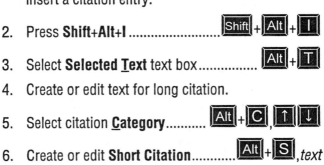

7. Click | **M**ark | .... Alt + M
   to mark single occurrence of citation.

   OR

   Click | **Mark All** | .... Alt + A
   to mark all occurrences of short
   and long citation in document.

   To mark additional citations in the document:

   a. Click | **Next Citation** | .... Alt + N

   b. Repeat steps 2–7.

8. Click | **Close** | .... Esc

Compile Table of Authorities

1. Place cursor in document where you want to insert
   table of authorities.

2. Select **I**nsert, Inde**x** and Tables ..... Alt + I , X

3. Select **Table of Authorities** tab .... Alt + A

4. Select desired........................... Alt + T , ↑ ↓
   table of authorities **Forma**t**s**.

5. Choose desired options.

6. Select **Category**...................... Alt + G , ↑ ↓
   for which to compile citations.

7. Select **Ta**b **Leader**.................. Alt + B , ↑ ↓

8. Click | **OK** | .... ↵

Proofing Tools

ANNOTATIONS

Annotations are used for inserting comments into a document by different reviewers. Annotation marks appear in a document as hidden text, consisting of the reviewer's initials and a number.

Annotations can be printed with the document or by themselves.

Insert Annotations

1. Place cursor at position in document where you want to insert annotation.

2. Press **Ctrl+Alt+A**.......................... `Ctrl`+`Alt`+`A`

   *NOTE: An annotation mark, consisting of the reviewer's initials and a number, will be inserted, and the **Annotations** pane appears.*

3. Type annotation text .... *text*

4. Click [**Close**] .... `Shift`+`Alt`+`C`
   to close **Annotations** pane.

Display Annotations

1. Double–click annotation mark in document.

2. Select **From** drop–down list box............ `Alt`+`R`

3. Select reviewer .... `↑` `↓`
   whose annotations you want
   displayed (default is **All Reviewers**).

4. Click [**Close**] .... `Shift`+`Alt`+`C`
   to close Annotations pane.

Delete Annotations

1. Select annotation mark to delete.

2. Press **Delete** .... Del

AUTOCORRECT

1. Place your cursor anywhere in document, or select text you want to use as an AutoCorrect.

2. Select **Tools**, **AutoCorrect** .... Alt + T, A

3. Choose desired **AutoCorrect** options.

4. Click OK .... ↵

GRAMMAR

> NOTE: Word will also spell check the document or selected text as it is performing a grammar check if the option is selected in the **Grammar** tab under **Tools**, **Options**.

1. Place cursor in document where you want to begin grammar check, or select desired text.

2. Select **Tools**, **Grammar** .... Alt + T, G

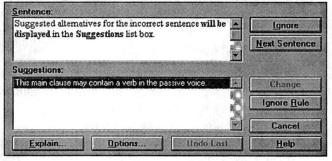

GRAMMAR (CONTINUED)

NOTE: Word appears incorrect sentences in the
Sentence list box. You can edit the
sentence displayed. Suggested
alternatives for the incorrect sentence will
be displayed in the Suggestions list box.

To choose alternate grammar suggestion:

Select grammar suggestion ..... `Alt` + `G` , `↑` `↓`

3. Choose desired button command for each error.

4. Click `[ Cancel ]` .... `Esc`
   to exit without making any changes.

   OR

   Click `[ Close ]` .... `Esc`
   to exit after making desired changes.

HYPHENATION

1. Select **Tools, Hyphenation** .... `Alt` + `T` , `H`

2. Choose desired hyphenation options.

3. Enter **Hyphenation Zone** .... `Alt` + `Z` , *number*
   (default is 0.25").

4. Select **Limit Consecutive** .... `Alt` + `L`
   Hyphens To scroll box.

5. Type number .... *number*
   for maximum number of lines that can
   end in hyphens (default is **No Limit**).

6. Click `[ OK ]` .... `↵`

To hyphenate document manually:

a. Click ⬚ **Manual...** .... ⬚ Alt +⬚ M

b. Click mouse to change hyphen position.

c. Click ⬚ **Yes** .... ⬚ Alt +⬚ Y
   to hyphenate word at selected position.

   OR

   Click ⬚ **No** .... ⬚ Alt +⬚ N
   to skip current word and move
   to next word to hyphenate.

PROTECT DOCUMENT

*Word documents can be protected to allow reviewers to make
comments on a document but not revisions by protecting it for
annotations. Documents can also be protected to allow
reviewers to make marked revisions only, which you can later
review. In addition, documents can also be protected to allow
only form fields to be filled.*

Protect Document

1. Select **Tools, Protect Document** .... ⬚ Alt +⬚ T ,⬚ P

2. Choose desired **Protect Document For** option.

   To protect specific sections of form:

   a. Click ⬚ **Sections...** .... ⬚ Alt +⬚ S

   *NOTE: This option is only available if **Forms** was
           selected in step 2.*

   b. Select **Protected Sections** .... ⬚ Alt +⬚ P

   c. Select sections............ ⬚ ↑ ⬚ ↓ then ⬚ Space
      to protect.

PROTECT DOCUMENT (CONTINUED)

    d.   Click `OK` .... `⏎`
        to close **Section Protection** dialog box.

To assign optional password:

Type **Password** .... `Alt`+`P`, *password*
to use to protect document.

3.   Click `OK` .... `⏎`

Unprotect Document

1.   Select **Tools**, **Unprotect Document** ...... `Alt`+`T`,`P`

    NOTE: If a password was selected with the
            Protect Document *command, above, the*
            Unprotect Document *dialog box appears,*
            prompting you for the selected password.

2.   Type appropriate password .... *password*

3.   Click `OK` .... `⏎`

REVISIONS

Turn Revisions On/Off

    NOTE: When revision marks are turned on, the
            MRK *message in the status bar will be*
            bold.

1.   Double–click `MRK` in status bar ..... `Alt`+`T`,`V`

2.   Choose desired **Document Revisions** option.

To select how revision marks will display:

Click `Options...` .... `Alt`+`O`

3.   Click `OK` .... `⏎`

WORD

Accept/Reject Revisions

Double–click ⬚MRK⬚ in status bar .... `Alt`+`T`, `V`

To accept all document revisions:

a. Click ⬚ **Accept All** ⬚ .... `Alt`+`A`

b. Click ⬚ **Yes** ⬚ .... `Alt`+`Y`
   when confirmation dialog box appears.

To reject all document revisions:

a. Click ⬚ **Reject All** ⬚ .... `Alt`+`J`

b. Click ⬚ **Yes** ⬚ .... `Alt`+`Y`
   when confirmation dialog box appears.

Compare Versions

Compares two versions of a document, inserting revision marks where a revised document differs from the original.

1. Double–click ⬚MRK⬚ in status bar .... `Alt`+`T`, `V`

2. Click ⬚ **Compare Versions...** ⬚ .... `Alt`+`C`

*The **Compare Versions** dialog box appears. If the name of the file you want to compare appears in the **Original File Name** text box, proceed to step 8.*

3. Select **List Files of Type** list box............ `Alt`+`T`

4. Select file type to compare .... `↑` `↓`

5. Select **Drives** drop–down list box .... `Alt`+`V`

6. Type or select drive letter .... *drive* or `↑` `↓`
   containing file to compare.

COMPARE VERSIONS (CONTINUED)

7. Double–click directory in **Directories** list box containing file to compare.

8. Double–click file in **Original File Name** list box.

> NOTE: If the revised document contains revision marks, you will receive a prompt, informing you Word may not be able to detect some of the existing revisions. Remove the revision marks with the procedures described in **Accept/Reject Revisions**, above.

Merge Revisions

Merges revisions and annotations from an open, revised document into the original document.

1. Double–click ⌧MRK in status bar ..... `Alt`+`T`,`V`

2. Click ⌈ **Merge Revisions...** ⌋ .... `Alt`+`E`

The Merge Revisions dialog box appears. If the name of the file you want to merge appears in the Original File Name text box, proceed to step 8.

3. Select **List Files of Type** list box .... `Alt`+`T`

4. Select file type to merge ....`↑``↓`

5. Select **Drives** drop–down list box.......... `Alt`+`V`

6. Type/select drive letter................. *drive* or `↑``↓` containing file to merge.

7. Double–click directory in **Directories** list box containing file to merge.

8. Double–click file in **Original File Name** list box.

SPELLING

> *NOTE:* *Various spell checking options can be*
> *selected in the **Spelling** tab under **Tools**,*
> ***Options**.*

1. Place cursor in document to spell check, or select
    desired text.

2. Click 🗹 .... `F7`

*The **Spelling** dialog box appears. Word appears misspelled*
*words in the **Not in Dictionary** text box. Suggested*
alternatives for the misspelled word will be displayed in the
Suggestions list box.

To choose alternative suggested word:

Select desired word in **Suggestions** ... `Alt`+`N`, `↑` `↓`

To select word not included in Suggestions list box:

Type replacement word .... `Alt`+`T`, *word*

3. Choose desired button command for each spelling
    error.

To change dictionary to which you want to add
unrecognized words:

Select dictionary .... `Alt`+`W`, `↑` `↓`

4. Click ▏ **Cancel** ▏ .... `Esc`
    to exit without making any changes.

5. Click ▏ **Close** ▏ .... `Esc`
    to exit after making desired changes.

THESAURUS

1. Select word or phrase for which you want to find synonym, antonym or related word.

2. Press **Shift+F7** .... `Shift`+`F7`

   To look up definition for word:

   a. Select **M**eanings .... `Alt`+`M`, `↑``↓`

   b. Click `Look Up` .... `Alt`+`L`

   To look up synonym for word or phrase displayed in Looked Up drop-down list box:

   a. Select **Replace with S**ynonym .... `Alt`+`S`

   b. Select synonym............................. `↑``↓`

   c. Click `Look Up` .... `Alt`+`L`

   To select different word looked up during current thesaurus session:

   Select desired word/phrase ..... `Alt`+`K`, `↑``↓`

3. Click to replace word or phrase .... `Alt`+`R`

WORD COUNT

1. Select **Tools, W**ord Count.............. `Alt`+`T`, `W`

The **Word Count** *dialog box appears with counted statistics for the active document.*

2. Select **Include F**ootnotes & Endnotes ... `Alt`+`F` to include footnotes and endnotes.

3. Click `Close` .... `Esc`

WORD

MAIL OPTIONS
ENVELOPES AND LABELS
Create Envelope

1. Select delivery address contained in current
    document. If current document does not contain
    address to print, leave cursor as flashing insertion
    point.

2. Select **Tools**, **Envelopes and Labels** **Alt** + **T**, **E**

3. Select [**Envelopes**] .... **Alt** + **E**

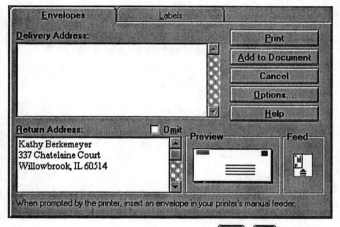

4. Type **Delivery Address** .... **Alt** + **D**, *address*
    or make desired edits to address selected in step 1.

    *NOTE: By default, Word uses the mailing address
    in the **User Info** tab of the **Options** dialog
    box as the return address.*

    #### To select different return address:

    Type **Return Address** .... **Alt** + **R**, address
    or make desired changes to default address.

64 WORD

CREATE ENVELOPE (CONTINUED)

To omit return address from envelope:

Select **O_mit** check box .... `Alt`+`M`

5. Click `Print` .... `Alt`+`P`

OR

Click `Add to Document` .... `Alt`+`A`

> *NOTE:* *If you made any changes to the return address, a prompt appears, asking if you want to save the new return address as the default.*

Envelope Options

1. Select **T_ools, E_nvelopes and Labels** `Alt`+`T`,`E`

2. Select `Envelopes` .... `Alt`+`E`

3. Click `Options...` .... `Alt`+`O`

4. Select `Envelope Options` .... `Alt`+`E`

5. Select **Envelope S_ize** .... `Alt`+`S`, `↑``↓`

6. Choose desired **If Mailed in the USA** option.

> *NOTE:* *This option is only available if **Delivery Point Bar Code** is selected.*

To change fonts for delivery and return addresses:

a. Click `Font...` .... `Alt`+`F`
to change delivery/return address font.

b. Select desired font.

To change delivery address placement:

a. Select **From Left** scroll box............. `Alt`+`L`

   OR

   Select **From Top** scroll box............. `Alt`+`T`

b. Type number for distance..................... *number*
   from edge of page (default is **Auto**).

To change return address placement:

a. Select **From Left** scroll box............. `Alt`+`M`

   OR

   Select **From Top** scroll box............. `Alt`+`R`

b. Type number for distance..................... *number*
   from edge of page (default is **Auto**).

7. Click [**OK**] .... `↵`

Printing Options

1. Select **Tools, Envelopes and Labels** `Alt`+`T`, `E`

2. Select [**Envelopes**] .... `Alt`+`E`

3. Click [**Options...**] .... `Alt`+`O`

4. Select [**Printing Options**] .... `Alt`+`P`

5. Choose desired **Feed Method** .... `Tab`, `↑` `↓`

6. Select **Feed From** drop–down list box ... `Alt`+`F`

PRINTING OPTIONS (CONTINUED)

7. Select printer tray .... ⬆️⬇️
   to use to feed envelopes into printer.

To return Printing Options tab to settings proposed by Word:

Click [__Reset__] .... `Alt`+`R`

8. Click [__OK__] .... `↵`

Create Labels

1. Select address contained in current document. If current document does not contain address to print, leave cursor as flashing insertion point.

2. Select **Tools, Envelopes and Labels** `Alt`+`T`,`E`

3. Select [__Labels__] .... `Alt`+`L`

4. Type **Address** list box .... `Alt`+`D`,*address*
   or make any edits to address selected in step **1**.

To use name and address stored in User Info tab of Options dialog box:

Select **Use Return Address** .... `Alt`+`R`

5. Select **Delivery Point Bar Code** .... `Alt`+`B`
    to print POSTNET (Postal Numeric
    Encoding Technique) bar code.

6. Select **Full Page of the Same Label** ...... `Alt`+`F`
    OR

    a. Select **Single Label** .... `Alt`+`N`

    b. Select **Row** or **Column** .... `Alt`+`W`/`C`

    c. Enter number of rows or columns .... *number*

7. Click | **Print** | .... `Alt`+`P`
    OR
    Click | **New Document** | .... `Alt`+`D`

    *NOTE: This option is unavailable if **Single Label** was selected in previous step.*

Label Options

1. Select **Tools, Envelopes and Labels**.... `Alt`+`T`, `E`

2. Select | Labels | .... `Alt`+`L`

3. Click | Options... | .... `Alt`+`O`

LABEL OPTIONS (CONTINUED)

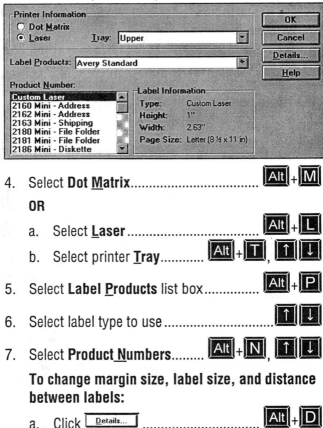

4. Select **Dot Matrix**.................................. ![Alt]+![M]

   OR

   a. Select **Laser** .... ![Alt]+![L]

   b. Select printer **Tray**........... ![Alt]+![T], ![↑]![↓]

5. Select **Label Products** list box............... ![Alt]+![P]

6. Select label type to use ....![↑]![↓]

7. Select **Product Numbers**........ ![Alt]+![N], ![↑]![↓]

   To change margin size, label size, and distance between labels:

   a. Click ▭ Details... .... ![Alt]+![D]

The Custom Label Information dialog box appears. The title of the dialog box changes to reflect the selected type of label.

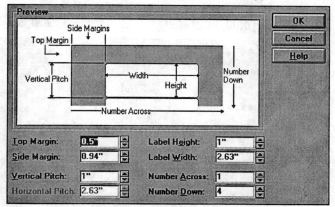

Top Margin:	0.5"	Label Height:	1"
Side Margin:	0.94"	Label Width:	2.63"
Vertical Pitch:	1"	Number Across:	1
Horizontal Pitch:	2.63"	Number Down:	4

EXAMPLE OF LABEL DEFINITION

NOTE: Several of the options in the Custom Label Information dialog box are not available for all label types.

   b. Choose desired dimensions to change.

   c. Type number for new dimension. .... *number*

8. Click ⬛ **OK** ⬛ .... ⏎

MAIL MERGE

Creating a mail merge involves several steps: creating the main document, creating the data source, inserting merge fields into the main document; then merging the two completed documents together.

Set Up Main Document

NOTE: This command is also used to restore a mail merge main document to a normal Word document.

SET UP MAIN DOCUMENT (CONTINUED)

1. Open document to use for the mail merge main document.

2. Select **Tools, Mail Merge** .... Alt + T , R

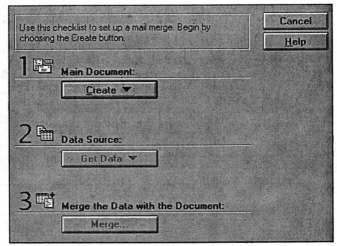

3. Click [Create ▼] .... Alt + C

4. Choose desired main document type.

   NOTE: This option is only available if the active document is a mail merge main document.

A prompt appears, asking if you want to use the active window or create a new document to use as the mail merge main document.

5. Click [**Active Window**] .... Alt + A

   OR

   Click [**New Main Document**] .... Alt + N

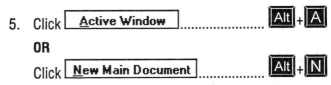

6. Click **Close** .... Esc
   to return to mail merge main document.

   OR

   Follow **Attach Data Source** procedures, below.

Mail Merge Toolbar

After creating a mail merge main document, the Mail Merge toolbar appears. Button names appear when you place the cursor on the desired button; a description of the button's functions appears in the status bar at the lower left corner of the screen.

Attach Data Source

Creates a new data source or opens an existing one. This command also allows you to specify a separate header row file for the data source. A header row is the top row in a data source table containing merge fields which identify the various types of information contained in the data source.

Create Data Source

1. Follow procedures under **Set Up Main Document**, page 69.

2. Select **Tools, Mail Merge** .... Alt + T , R

3. Click **Get Data ▼** .... Alt + G

   NOTE: This option is unavailable if active Word document has not been set up as a mail merge main document.

4. Select **Create Data Source** C

CREATE DATA SOURCE (CONTINUED)

> *NOTE: Commonly used field names will be listed in the **Field Names in Header Row** list box.*

A mail merge data source is composed of rows of data. The first row is called the header row. Each of the columns in the header row begins with a field name.

Word provides commonly used field names in the list below. You can add or remove field names to customize the header row.

Field Name:

Field Names in Header Row:

Title
FirstName
LastName
JobTitle
Company
Address1
Address2

Add Field Name ▶▶

Remove Field Name

Move

OK   Cancel   MS Query...   Help

To add field names:

a. Type **Field Name** .... `Alt`+`F`, *field name*

b. Click ⌐ **Add Field Name ▶▶** ⌐ ...... `Alt`+`A`

To remove field names:

a. To remove **Field Names** .... `Alt`+`N`, `↑` `↓`
   in Header Row

b. Click ⌐ **Remove Field Name** ⌐ .... `Alt`+`R`

To reorder field names:

a. To move **Field Names** ...... `Alt`+`N`, `↑` `↓`
   in Header Row

b. Click `↑` or `↓`

5. Click ⌐ **OK** ⌐ .... `↵`

6. Follow procedures under **SAVE FILE**, page 8.

CREATE DATA SOURCE (CONTINUED)

After saving the data source file, a prompt appears, asking if
you want to edit the data source or the main document.

7. Click ⎡   **Edit Data Source** ⎤ .... `Alt`+`D`

> NOTE: The field names selected in step 5 appear
>   in the **Field Names** list box.

To add new records:

a. Click mouse button to move between field
    names text boxes in **Field Name** list box.

    OR

    Press **Tab** or **Shift+Tab**..... `Tab` or `Shift`+`Tab`

b. Type information..................................... . *text*
    into selected field name text boxes.

c. Click ⎡   **Add New** ⎤ .... `Alt`+`A`

d. Repeat steps a–c to add additional records.

To move between records:
Click desired record button.

8. Choose desired button option:

*   ⎡   **Delete** ⎤ .... `Alt`+`D`
    to remove selected record from data source.

*   ⎡   **Restore** ⎤ .... `Alt`+`F`
    to restore selected record to its original
    contents.

*   ⎡   **Find...** ⎤ .... `Alt`+`F`
    to search data source for specified information.

*   ⎡   **View Source** ⎤ .... `Alt`+`V`
    to view data source file in table form.

CREATE DATA SOURCE (CONTINUED)

> *NOTE: Viewing data source file allows you to edit data records using the **Database** toolbar.*

9. Click [OK] .... [↵]

Open Data Source

1. Follow **Set Up Main Document** procedure, page 69.

2. Select **Tools, Mail Merge** .... [Alt]+[T],[R]

3. Click [**Get Data ▼**] .... [Alt]+[G]

> *NOTE: This option is unavailable if the active Word document has not been set up as a mail merge main document.*

4. Select **Open Data Source** .... [O]

5. Follow **OPEN FILE** procedure, page 7.

Insert Merge Fields into Main Document

1. Place cursor in mail merge main document where **you** want to insert merge field.

2. Press **Shift+Alt+F** .... [Shift]+[Alt]+[F]

Mail Merge Fields:	Word Fields:	
Title	Ask...	OK
FirstName	Fill-in...	Cancel
LastName	If...Then	Help
JobTitle	If...Then...Else	
Company	Merge Record #	
Address1	Next Record	
Address2	Next Record If	

3. Select **Mail Merge Fields** .... [Alt]+[M], [↑][↓]

4. Select desired **Word Fields** .... [Alt]+[W], [↑][↓]

5. Repeat steps 1–4 to insert additional merge fields.

6. Click [OK] .... [↵]

Merge Main Document and Data Source

Merges the main document and attached data source with the Tools, Mail Merge command.

1. Click 🔲 .... Alt+T , R , Alt+M
   in Mail Merge toolbar.

2. Select **Merge To** drop–down list box ..... Alt+R

3. Select **New Document** or **Printer** .... ↑ ↓

4. Select **All** .... Alt+A
   to merge all records in data source.

   OR

   a. Select **From** text box .... Alt+F

   b. Type number .... *number*
      of first record in range or records to merge.

   c. Select **To** text box .... Alt+T

   d. Type number .... *number*
      of last record in range or records to merge.

5. Choose desired **When Merging Records** option.

6. Click ⎣ **Check Errors...** ⎦ .... Alt+E

7. Select desired error checking option.

8. Click ⎣ **OK** ⎦ .... ↵

   To select query options for mail merge:

   Click ⎣ **Query Options...** ⎦ .... Alt+Q

9. Click ⎣ **Merge** ⎦ .... ↵

COMPOUND DOCUMENTS

A ***compound document*** *refers to a document that has been created with information from more than one application. For example, a compound document can contain data from graphic, spreadsheet, and database programs.*

DRAWING TOOLS

Create/Edit Graphic Items

—FROM PRINT PREVIEW OR PAGE LAYOUT VIEW—

1. Click  on standard toolbar.

The Drawing toolbar appears.

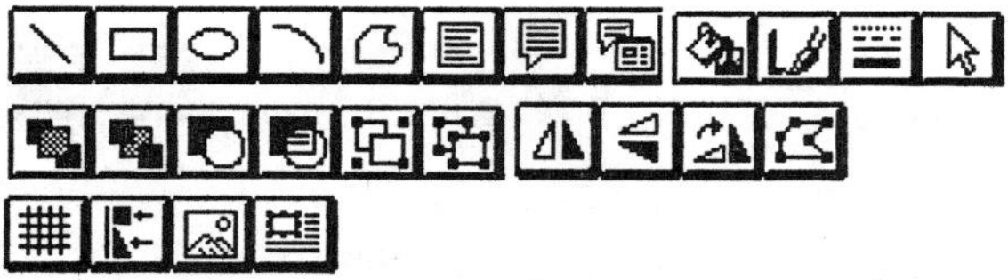

2. Create and edit graphic items using tools from Drawing toolbar.

Create Picture

1. Place cursor in document where you want to create a new picture.
2. Click  on Drawing toolbar.
3. Create and edit graphic items using tools from Drawing toolbar.

   To adjust picture boundaries to fit graphic items:

   Click  on Picture toolbar.

   To close picture and return to document:

   Click [Close Picture] .... Alt + C
   on Picture toolbar.

Edit Picture

NOTE:　An imported graphic modified with this command will be converted to a Word 6.0 Picture object. Any links with external files will be broken.

1. Double–click Word 6.0 Picture object or imported graphic to edit.

2. Create and edit graphic items using tools from Drawing toolbar.

   To adjust picture boundaries to fit graphic items:

   Click ⊞ on Picture toolbar.

   To close picture and return to document:

   Click [Close Picture] .... Alt + C
   on Picture toolbar.

EMBEDDED OBJECTS

*An embedded object is information created in another application, yet entirely self–contained within a Word document. Although not linked to any external files, embedded objects can be edited and updated in their source applications from within Word. In addition to the following procedures, embedded objects can also be created with the **Paste Special** command.*

Create New Embedded Objects

1. Select **I**nsert, **O**bject .... Alt + I , O

2. Select [**C**reate New] .... Alt + C

3. Select **O**bject Type list box.................... Alt + O

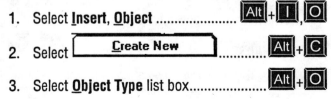

CREATE NEW EMBEDDED OBJECTS (CONTINUED)

4. Select application.......................... ⬆⬇
   from which to create object.

5. Select **Display as Icon** check box.......... Alt+A
   to display object as icon in document.

   To change icon representing embedded object:

   a. Click ⌐ **Change Icon...** ⌐ .... Alt+I

   *NOTE: This option is only available if **Display as**
   Icon check box has been selected.*

   b. Select desired **Icon**.......... Alt+I, ⬆⬇

   To search for other files that contain icons:

   Click ⌐ **Browse...** ⌐ .... Alt+B

   c. Select **Caption**........................Alt+C, *text*
      to change for selected icon.

   d. Click ⌐ **OK** ⌐ .... ↵
      to close **Change Icon** dialog box.

6. Click ⌐ **OK** ⌐ to create .... ↵

7. Create desired information.

8. Select **File**, **Update** .... Alt+F, U
   from within the application.

9. Press **Alt+F4** .... Alt+N

   *NOTE: Ways of saving and exiting vary with
   different applications.*

Edit Embedded Object

1. Double–click object to edit.

*The name of the **Object** command changes depending on the selected object (e.g., **Excel Worksheet Object, Paintbrush Picture Object**, etc.).*

> *NOTE: The selected object opens in its originating application.*

2. Make desired edits

3. Select **File, Update**........................ `Alt`+`F`,`U`
   from within the application.

4. Press **Alt+F4**.. `Alt`+`N`

> *NOTE: Ways of saving and exiting vary with different applications. Steps 3–4 are generic procedures for saving and exiting in many applications, but not all. For more information, see the documentation for the applications you are using.*

FORMAT PICTURE

Format Picture

1. Select graphic whose size, scaling or cropping you want to change.

2. Select **Format, Picture** .... `Alt`+`O`,`R`

*The **Picture** dialog box appears. The original dimensions of the selected graphic are displayed in the **Original Size** box.*

3. Choose desired **Crop From** option.

> *NOTE: If you select **Bottom** in the step above, enter number for crop dimension.*

4. Choose desired **Scaling** option and enter scaling percentage.

FORMAT PICTURE (CONTINUED)

> *NOTE: Any changes to scaling options are also reflected in size options, below.*

5. Choose desired **Size** option and enter size.

> *NOTE: Any changes to size options are also reflected in scaling options, above.*

To remove cropping and return graphic to its original size:

Click [Re**s**et] .... Alt + S

To format frame for selected graphic:

Click [Frame...] .... Alt + F

> *NOTE: The **Frame** button is only available if a frame has been added to the selected graphic.*

6. Click [OK] .... ↵

Size and Scale Graphic

1.   Click graphic to size and scale.

*Sizing handles appear on the top, bottom, right, and left edges,
and in each corner of the selected graphic. The sizing handles
in the corners resize the graphic proportionally, while the
sizing handles on the top, bottom, left, and right edges resize
the graphic vertically and horizontally.*

2.   Move mouse on top of sizing handle until pointer
     changes to ↔

3.   Hold mouse button, drag to desired size and
     release mouse button.

Crop Graphic

1.   Click graphic to crop.

*Sizing handles appear on the top, bottom, right, and left edges,
and in each corner of the selected graphic. The sizing handles
in the corners crop the graphic proportionally, while the sizing
handles on the top, bottom, left, and right edges crop the
graphic vertically and horizontally.*

2.   Hold **Shift** ....

CROP GRAPHIC (CONTINUED)

3. Move mouse on top of sizing handle until pointer changes to a ⛶

4. Hold mouse button, drag to desired size and release mouse button.

INSERT FILE

Inserts files or sections of files into the current document. Files can be other Word documents or from other applications.

1. Select **I**nsert, Fi**l**e .... [Alt]+[I],[L]

2. Select **List Files of Type** .... [Alt]+[T], [↑][↓] to insert.

    If you want to be prompted before Word converts file types from other applications:

    Select **C**onfirm Conversions .... [Alt]+[C]

3. Select **Dri**v**es** drop–down list box .... [Alt]+[V]

4. Type or select drive letter .... *drive* or [↑][↓] containing file you want to insert.

5. Double–click directory in **Directories** list box containing file to insert.

6. Select **L**ink to File check box .... [Alt]+[L] to link selected file to its source.

    > *NOTES: Selecting the **Link to File** check box inserts an **INCLUDE** field into the document*

7. Double–click file in **File N**ame list box.

INSERT PICTURE

Inserts pictures and graphics from other applications into the current document, as well as the various clip art files that come with Word.

1. Select **I**nsert, **P**icture .... `Alt`+`I`,`P`

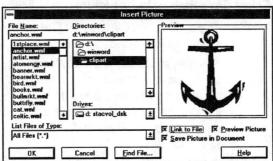

2. Select **List Files of Type** list box............ `Alt`+`T`

3. Select graphic file type .... `↑` `↓`
   (See your Word documentation or on–line Help for a listing of graphic file types that can be opened in Word.)

4. Select drive................. `Alt`+`V`, *drive* or `↑` `↓` containing graphic file to insert.

5. Double–click directory in **Directories** list box containing graphic file to insert.

6. Select **Preview Picture** check box.......... `Alt`+`P` to preview graphic file before inserting it into document.

7. Select **Link to File** check box .... `Alt`+`L` to link selected graphic file to its source.

INSERT PICTURE (CONTINUED)

*NOTE: Selecting the **Link to File** check box inserts*
*an **INCLUDE** field into the document.*

To store graphic in Word document along
with link:

Select **Save Picture in Document**..........

*NOTES: This option is only available if **Link to File***
check box is selected.

*Selecting the **Save Picture in Document***
check box increases the size of the Word
file since a complete representation of the
graphic is stored in the document.
Deselect this check box to decrease the
size of the Word file.

8.   Double–click file in **File Name** list box.

MANAGE WORKBOOKS

Create New Workbook
Click 🗋 .... `Ctrl`+`N`
to open new workbook based on default template.

Open Existing Workbook
1. Click 📂 .... `Ctrl`+`O`
2. Select desired workbook(s) to open.

   NOTES: You can select multiple files by holding
   ***Ctrl** while clicking each file you want to*
   *open in **File Name** list box.*

   If you open a template file, Excel will open
   a copy of the file and add a number to the
   end of its workbook name.

3. Click **OK** .... `↵`

Hide Workbook
Hides a workbook from view, but does not close it.

1. Select workbook to hide.
2. Select **W**indow, **H**ide .... `Alt`+`W`,`H`

Unhide Workbook
1. Select **W**indow, **U**nhide .... `Alt`+`W`,`U`
2. Select workbook to unhide in **Unhide Workbook**
   list.
3. Click **OK** .... `↵`

Close Active Workbook Window(s)

Click ⊟ .... Alt + F , C

OR

Press **Shift, File, Close All** .... Shift + Alt + F , C

> *NOTE: If you have not saved changes made to the
> workbook, Excel will prompt you to save
> them.*

Save Previously Saved Active Workbook

Click 🖫 .... Alt + F , S

> *NOTE: The **Save As** dialog box will appear if you
> have not previously saved the file, or if you
> opened the file as read–only.*

Save Active Workbook As

1. Click **File, Save As** .... Alt + F , A

2. Select drive or directory in which file will be saved.

3. Type filename .... *filename*

4. Click ▎▔▔**OK**▔▔▏ .... ↵

Save Workspace

1. Click **File, Save Workspace** .... Alt + F , W

2. Select drive or directory in which workspace file
   will be saved.

3. Type filename .... *filename*

4. Click ▎▔▔**OK**▔▔▏ .... ↵

EXCEL

Set General Workbook Options

1. Select **Tools**, **Options**... .... `Alt`+`T`,`O`

2. Select ⌐ General ⌐ .... `←` `→` `↑` `↓`

3. Select desired options.

4. Select ⌐ **OK** ⌐ .... `↵`

Select Sheets in Workbooks

*By default, new workbooks contain worksheets labeled Sheet1,
Sheet2 etc. You can delete, rename, move, copy, and hide
sheets. You can also insert sheets of the following types:
Worksheet, Chart, MS Excel 4.0 Macro, Module, and Dialog.
Select Sheets selects the following sheet types: Worksheet,
Chart, MS Excel 4.0 Macro, Module, and Dialog.*

> *NOTE: You select sheets by selecting their sheet
> tabs, located on the bottom of the
> workbook window. Selected sheet tabs are
> white, the active sheet tab is bold. Use the
> tab scrolling buttons (illustrated below) to
> view hidden sheet tabs. If no sheets are
> visible, see Set View Options, page 138.*

Select `\Sheet# /` ....*sheet #*

To select all sheets:

a. Right–click any `\Sheet# /` ....*sheet #*

b. Select **Select All Sheets**.

To select (group) consecutive sheets:

> *IMPORTANT: When you group worksheets,
> entries and formatting applied to
> one worksheet are duplicated on all
> worksheets in the group.*

SELECT SHEETS IN WORKBOOKS (CONTINUED)

  a. Select any `\Sheet#/` .... *sheet #*

  b. Press **Shift** and click .... Shift , *sheet #'s*

To select (group) non–consecutive sheets:
IMPORTANT: When you group worksheets,
entries and formatting applied to
one worksheet are duplicated on all
worksheets in the group.

  a. Select first `\Sheet#/` .... *sheet #*

  b. Press **Ctrl** and click each sheet .. Ctrl +*sheet #'s*

Deselect Grouped Sheets

Click `\Sheet#/` of any sheet that is *not* in group.

OR

  a. Right–click name of `\Sheet#/` in group.

  b. Select **Ungroup Sheets**.

Hide/Unhide Sheet

NOTE: If a workbook has only one sheet, the
sheet can not be hidden.

1. Select sheet to hide/unhide.

2. Select **Format**, **Sheet** .... Alt + O H

3. Select **Hide**/ **Unhide** .... H / U

Insert Sheets

1. Right–click `\Sheet#/` in front of sheet where new
    sheet will be inserted.

2. Select **Insert** .... ↑ ↓ , ⏎

3. Select type of sheet to insert in **New** list ... 【↑】【↓】

   *NOTE: If chart was selected, follow the
            ChartWizard prompts.*

4. Select [OK] .... ⏎

Delete Sheets

1. Right–click \Sheet#/ to delete.

2. Select **Delete**.

3. Select [OK] .... ⏎

Rename Sheet

1. Double–click name of sheet .... *name of sheet*

2. Type new name in **Name** box....................... *name*

3. Click [OK] .... ⏎

Move Sheets Within Workbook

Drag \Sheet#/ to desired tab location.

Pointer becomes a ⬚, and black triangle indicates point of insertion.

Copy Sheets Within Workbook

NOTE: Excel will rename sheets that you copy.

Press **Ctrl** and drag \Sheet#/ to desired tab position.

Pointer changes to ⬚, and black triangle indicates point of insertion.

Select Cells

To select one cell:
Select cell.

To select range of cells:
Drag to highlight desired cells.

To select multiple selection of cells:
a. Select first cell.

b. Press **Ctrl** and click each additional cell.
   AND/OR
   Press **Ctrl** and drag to highlight desired cells.

To select entire row/column
Select row or column heading.

To select adjacent rows or columns:
Point to first row or column heading, click and drag through desired rows or columns.

To select all cells in worksheet:
Select **Select All** button ▦ located at intersection of row and column headings.

To deselect any cell selection:
Select any cell.

To select row/column in data block:
*NOTE: A **data block** is a group of adjacent cells containing data.*

a. Select first cell(s) in block.

b. Point to border of selected cell(s) in direction to extend selection.

c. Press **Shift** and double–click selection border.

To select named reference from Name box:
Select name in **Name box** to left of the formula bar.

EXCEL

EXCEL

To select cell reference from Name box:

a. Select in **Name box** to left of formula bar.

b. Type cell reference.

c. Select [OK] .... ⏎

NOTE: You can also select specific cells by selecting Go To from the Edit menu.

To select (go to) named or specific cell reference:

a. Press **F5** F5

b. Enter cell reference name in **Reference** box or select from **Go to**.

c. Select [OK] .... ⏎

Select Cells Containing Special Contents

1. Select cells to search.

2. Select **Edit**, **Go To** F5

3. Select **Special** .... Alt + S

4. Select desired **Go To Special** options.

   NOTE: If Precedents or Dependents was selected, Excel searches the entire worksheet.

5. Select [OK] .... ⏎

Cell Selection Keys

TO:	PRESS:
Select single cell	← → ↑ ↓
Extend selection in direction of arrow	Shift + ← → ↑ ↓
Extend selection to beginning of row	Shift + Home
Extend selection to end of data block in direction of arrow	End, Shift + ← → ↑ ↓
Select entire current row	Shift + Space
Select entire current column	Ctrl + Space
Select first cell in current row	Home
Select cell in current row in last occupied column	End + ↵
Select first cell in worksheet	Ctrl + Home
Select last cell containing data in worksheet	Ctrl + End
Extend selection to first cell in worksheet	Ctrl + Shift + Home
Extend selection to last cell containing data in worksheet	Ctrl + Shift + End
Select entire worksheet	Ctrl + A
Select first or last cell in a horizontal data block* or select first or last cell in row	Ctrl + ← (first) Ctrl + → (last)
Select first or last cell in a vertical data block* or select first or last cell in column	Ctrl + ↑ (first) Ctrl + ↓ (last)

EXCEL

CELL SELECTION KEYS (CONTINUED)

Extends selection to end of data block* in direction of arrow	`Ctrl` + `Shift` + `←` `→` `↑` `↓`
Extend selection to include entire data block*	`Ctrl` + `Shift` `*`
Extend selection up one screen	`Shift` + `Page Up`
Extend selection down one screen	`Shift` + `Page Down`
Deselect a multiple selection, except active cell	`Shift` + `Backspace`

*A **data block** is a group of adjacent cells containing data.

Enter Text

> NOTE: Text cannot be calculated. By default, text is left–aligned.

1. Select cell(s) to receive text.
2. Type text... *text*
3. Press **Enter**..`↵`

Enter Numbers as Text

> NOTE: Numbers entered as text cannot be calculated. By default, numbers entered as text are left–aligned.

1. Select cell(s) to receive data.
2. Press **'** (apostrophe)...`'`
3. Enter number ....*number*
4. Press **Enter**..`↵`

Enter Numbers as Values

*NOTE: Numbers can be calculated. By default,
numbers are right–aligned.*

1. Select cell(s) to receive numbers.

   To format number as currency:

   Press **$** .... 🔳$

2. Enter number... *number*

   *NOTE: Precede negative numbers with a minus
   sign (–), or enclose negative number
   within parentheses ().*

   To format number as percentage:

   Press **%** .... 🔳%

3. Press **Enter** .... ⏎

   *NOTES: If Excel displays ######, column is not
   wide enough to display the number. To
   change column width, see **Change Column
   Widths**, page 128. To change the format,
   see **Format Number/Date/Time**, page 133.*

Enter Numbers as Fractions

*NOTE: Numbers can be calculated. By default,
numbers are right–aligned.*

1. Select cell(s) to receive numbers.

2. Type **0** (zero) 0

3. Press **Enter** .... Space

4. Type fraction..*fraction*

   Example: 0 ¼

ENTER NUMBERS AS FRACTIONS (CONTINUED)

5. Press **Enter**.......................................

> *NOTE:* *If Excel displays ######, the column is not
> wide enough to display the date. To
> change column width, see **Change Column
> Widths**, page 128.*

Enter Date

> *NOTE:* *Date is a number and is right–aligned.*

1. Select cell to receive date.

To enter current date:

Press **Ctrl+;** (semi–colon) .... Ctrl + ;

To enter specific date:
Type date in valid format:

You may use the following formats:
m/d/yy   *(e.g. 6/24/52)*
d–mmm   *(e.g. 24–Jun)*
d–mmm–yy   *(e.g. 24–Jun–52)*
mmm–yy   *(e.g. Jun–52)*

2. Press **Enter**.......................................

> *NOTES:* *If Excel displays ######, column is not
> wide enough to display the date. To
> change column width, see **Change Column
> Widths**, page 128. To change the date
> format, see **Format Number/Date/Time**,
> page 133.*

Enter Time

> *NOTE:* *Time is a number and is right–aligned.*

1. Select cell to receive time.

ENTER TIME (CONTINUED)

To enter current time:

Press **Ctrl+Shift+:** (colon) ....

To enter specific time:

Type time in a valid format.

You may use the following formats:
h:mm:ss AM/PM   (e.g. 1.:55:25 PM)
h:mm AM/PM   (e.g. 1.:55 PM)
h:mm   (e.g. 1.:55)
h:mm:ss   (e.g. 1.:55:25)

2. Press **Enter** .... 🔲

> *NOTES: If Excel displays ######, column is not*
> *wide enough to display the date. To*
> *change column width, see **Change Column***
> ***Widths**, page 128. To change the time*
> *format, see **Format Number/Date/Time**,*
> *page 133.*

Cancel Cell Entry Before it is Entered

Click ⊠ .... Esc

Set Edit Options

1. Select **Tools, Options** ....

2. Select | Edit | ....

3. Select/deselect **Settings** options.

4. Select | OK | .... 🔲

Edit Cells

1. Double–click cell to edit................................... F2
   ☒ *Cancel* button—*cancels changes made in cell*
   ☑ *Enter* button— *accepts changes made in cell*
   fx *Function Wizard* button—*starts Function Wizard.*
2. Select anywhere in formula bar and make desired changes.
3. Press **Enter** to accept changes......................... ⏎

Copy Cell Contents

1. Select cell(s) to copy.
2. Select **E**dit, **C**opy .... Alt + E , C

A flashing outline surrounds selection.

To change destination workbook or worksheet:
Select workbook and/or sheet.

3. Select destination cell(s).

   *NOTE: Select an area the same size as the area to
   copy, or select the upper left cell in the
   destination cell range. To copy to multiple
   areas, press **Ctrl** and click upper left cell in
   each destination area.*

To copy once and overwrite existing data in destination cells:

Press **Enter**.. ⏎

To copy (with option to repeat copy) and overwrite existing data in destination cells:

a. Select **E**dit, **P**aste .... Alt + E , P

COPY CELL CONTENTS (CONTINUED)

To repeat copy:

i. Select upper left cell in destination area.

ii. Select **Edit, Paste** .... `Alt`+`E`,`P`

iii. Repeat steps a and b for each copy to make.

b. Press **Esc** to end copying.......................... `Esc`

To copy/insert between existing cells:

a. Select **Insert, Copied Cells** .... `Alt`+`I`,`E`

b. Select desired **Insert Paste** option, if prompted.

c. Select `      OK      ` .... `↵`

d. Press **Esc** to end copying.......................... `Esc`

Clear Cell Options

Removes the formats, contents (data and formulas), notes, or all the above, and leaves the cells blank in the worksheet. When cleared cells are referenced by formulas, they return a value of zero.

1. Select cell(s) to clear.

2. Select **Edit, Clear**.......................... `Alt`+`E`,`A`

3. Select desired **Clear** option.

Delete Cells

Removes the cells from the worksheet. Adjacent cells are shifted to close the space left by the deletion. When deleted cells are referenced by a formula, the formula will show a #REF! error message.

1. Select cell(s) to delete.

2. Select **Edit**, **Delete**... .... `Alt`+`E`,`D`

3. Select desired **Delete** option.

4. Select [**OK**] .... `⏎`

Delete Rows/Columns

> *NOTE:* *Deleting removes the rows or columns*
> *from the worksheet and shifts adjacent*
> *rows or columns into the space left by the*
> *deletion. When cells in the deleted rows or*
> *columns are referenced, a formula will*
> *show a #REF! error message.*

1. Select rows/columns to delete.

2. Select **Edit**, **Delete** .... `Alt`+`E`,`D`

Insert Blank Cells

Existing data is shifted to make room for inserted cells. Excel adjusts references to shifted cells.

1. Select cell(s) where insertion will occur.

> *NOTE:* *Select the same number of cells as the*
> *blank cells to insert.*

2. Select **Insert**, **Cells**......................... `Alt`+`I`,`E`

3. Select desired **Insert** option.

4. Select [**OK**] .... `⏎`

Insert Blank Rows/Columns

1. Select rows or columns where insertion will occur.

NOTE: Select the number of rows or columns you want to insert.

2. Select **I**nsert, **R**ows/**C**olumns..... Alt + I , R / C

Create Series of Numbers, Dates, Times

1. Enter first series value in a cell to base series on a single value.

   OR

   Enter first and second series values in consecutive cells to base series on multiple values.

2. Select cells containing series values and cells to fill.

   NOTE: Select adjacent cells in rows or columns to fill.

3. Select **E**dit, F**i**ll .... Alt + E , I

4. Select **S**eries .... S

5. Select desired options.

6. Select ⌐ OK ⌐ .... ↵

Spell Check

1. Select any cell to search entire sheet.

2. Select ABC button .... Alt + T , S

3. Select desired options.

4. Select ⌐ OK ⌐ .... ↵

Find and Replace Data

(See Find and Replace, page 25.)

FORMULAS AND FUNCTIONS

Enter New Formula

1. Select cell to receive formula.

2. Press **=** ....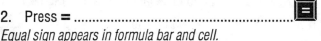

Equal sign appears in formula bar and cell.

3. Enter formula.

EXAMPLES: *=A1*(B2:B10)/2. =SUM(A1:A10)*5*

    NOTE: *For information about inserting references and functions into a formula, see* **Build Formula***, below.*

4. Press **Enter**..

Build Formula

Use these procedures to insert the following into a formula:

- *A cell reference from any workbook or worksheet.*
- *A named reference.*
- *A named formula.*
- *A function (using the Function Wizard).*

To insert cell reference:

a. If necessary, type or edit formula.

b. Place insertion point in formula where reference will be inserted.

NOTE: *If necessary, type preceding operator or left parenthesis [(].*

c. If necessary, select workbook and/or sheet containing cells to reference.

NOTE: *When you select a cell in another workbook, Excel creates a link to that workbook.*

d. Select cell or cell range to insert in formula.

Reference appears in formula bar and cell.

BUILD FORMULA (CONTINUED)

To enter 3.–D reference for range of worksheets:

Press **Shift** and click last worksheet tab to reference.

e. Type or build remaining parts of formula....

To insert named reference/named formula:

a. If necessary, type or edit formula.

b. Place insertion point where named reference or named formula will be inserted.

NOTE: If necessary, type preceding operator or left parenthesis [(].

c. Click <u>I</u>nsert, <u>N</u>ame, <u>P</u>aste..

d. Select reference or formula name in **Paste Name** list.

e. Click [OK] .... ⏎

f. Enter/build remaining parts of formula.

To insert worksheet function using Function Wizard:

*NOTE: You can also insert a function by selecting, **Function** from the <u>I</u>nsert menu.*

a. If necessary, type or edit formula.

b. Place insertion point where function will be inserted.

c. Click 📏 .... Shift + F3

Function Wizard—Step 1 of 2

d. Select category in **Function Category** list.

e. Select a function in **Function Name** list.

f. Click **Next >** .... ⏎

Function Wizard—Step 2 of 2

g. Type or insert arguments in argument boxes.

NOTE: *An argument is data you supply to a function so it can perform its operation.*

h. Click **Finish** .... Alt + F

i. Type or build remaining parts of formula.

Edit Worksheet Functions (Function Wizard)

1. Select cell containing function(s).

   NOTE: *Do not double–click cell.*

2. Click fx .... Shift + F3

3. Edit or add arguments in argument boxes.

   NOTE: *An argument is data you supply to a function so it can perform its operation.*

   To edit next or previous function in cell:

   a. Click **Next >** or **< Back**

   b. Edit or add arguments in argument boxes.

   c. Repeat steps a–b, as needed.

4. Click **Finish** .... Alt + F

Using Text in Titles to Name Cells

NOTE: *You must convert titles that are numbers to text. Excel converts date values to text automatically. Spaces in text are replaced with underscore characters in the reference name.*

1. Select cells containing titles for names and extend selection to include cells to name.

2. Click **Insert, Name, Create** ..... `Alt`+`I`,`N`,`C`

3. Select desired **Create Names in** options.

4. Click `OK` .... `↵`

Name Cell Reference (Using Name Box)

1. Select cell(s) to name.

2. Click **Name box** on left side of formula bar.

3. Type name for selected cell(s).

4. Press **Enter** .... `↵`

Name Formula or Value

1. Click **Insert, Name, Define** .... `Ctrl`+`F3`

2. Type name in **Names in Workbook** text box.

3. Click **Refers to** box.

4. Delete existing reference.

NOTE: *By default, Excel enters cell reference to selected cells in **Refers to** box.*

5. Type formula or value .... *formula/value*

NOTE: *Precede formula or value with an equal sign (=). Formula may be pasted from the Clipboard. Cell references may be entered in formula by selecting cells in worksheet.*

To add another named formula or value:

a. Click [**Add**]............................... `Alt`+`A`

b. Repeat steps 2–5.

6. Click [**OK**].. `↵`

Edit/View Named Cell Reference or Named Formula

1. Click **Insert**, **Name**, **Define**...... `Alt`+`I`, `N`, `D`

2. Select name to edit/view in **Names in Workbook** list.

Reference or formula appears in **Refers to** *text box.*

To change name:

a. Type new name in **Names in Workbook** list.

b. Click [**Add**]............................... `Alt`+`A`

c. Select old name in **Names in Workbook** list.

d. Click [**Delete**]........................... `Alt`+`D`

To change reference the name refers to:

a. Click **Refers to** text box.

b. If necessary, delete all or part of reference.

c. Select cells in worksheet to reference.

   OR

   Type new reference.

NOTE: Precede reference with an equal sign (=).

To change a named formula or value:

a. Click **Refers to** text box.

b. Edit formula or value.

NOTE: Precede formula or value with an equal sign (=). Formula may be pasted from the clipboard. Cell references may be entered in formula by selecting cells in worksheet.

3. Click [**OK**].. `↵`

Replace References with Defined Names

Excel searches worksheet for references that have been given names and replaces the references with the names.

1. Select any cell to replace all references with names in worksheet.

   OR

   Select cells containing reference to replace.

2. Click **Insert, Name, Apply** .... `Alt`+`I`,`N`,`A`

3. Select names in **Apply Names** list.

4. Select/deselect desired options.

   To set other options:

   a. Click `Options >>` .... `Alt`+`O`

   b. Select/deselect desired **Apply Names** options.

5. Click `OK` .... `↵`

Delete Named Cell References or Named Formulas

> *NOTE: Excel will display #NAME? error message in cells containing formulas referring to a deleted name.*

1. Click **Insert, Name, Define** ..... `Alt`+`I`,`N`,`D`

2. Select name to delete in **Names in Workbook** list.

3. Click `Delete` .... `Alt`+`D`

4. Click `OK` .... `↵`

AutoSum

1. Select cell(s) to receive sum(s).

   *NOTE: Select blank cell(s) below or to the right of
   cells containing values to total.*

   To automatically calculate grand totals:
   Select cells that include subtotals and a blank row
   and/or column adjacent to range.

2. Click Σ .... `Alt` + `=`

*Excel inserts =SUM() function in formula bar, and a flashing
outline may surround cells to be totaled.*

   To change proposed range to total:
   Select cells to total.

3. If necessary, press **Enter** to add numbers........ `⏎`

Calculate Only Selected Worksheet
(When Calculation is Set to Manual)

*Also updates charts embedded in worksheet and open chart
sheets linked to worksheet.*

1. Select worksheet to calculate.

2. Press **Shift+F9** .... `Shift` + `F9`

Calculate All Open Workbooks
(When Calculation is Set to Manual)

*Also updates all charts in open workbooks and calculates data
tables when Calculation is set to Automatic Except Tables.*

Press **F9**... `F9`

Create Link Between Workbooks

1. Open workbooks to link and arrange workspace so both workbooks are in view.

2. Select worksheet in source workbook containing cells to reference.

3. Select cell(s) to reference.

4. Click **Edit**, **Copy**.............................. `Alt`+`E`,`C`

5. Select worksheet in dependent workbook.

6. Select cell(s) to receive link.

   NOTE: If referencing more than one cell, select upper left cell in destination cell range.

   To paste link as values:

   a. Click **Edit**, **Paste Special** .... `Alt`+`E`,`S`

   b. Click `Paste Link` .... `Alt`+`L`

   If a reference includes more than one cell, Excel creates a single array formula in destination cells.

   To paste link as a picture:
   Press **Shift** and select **Edit**,

   Paste Picture Link.............. `Shift`+`Alt`+`E`,`N`

7. Press **Esc** to end procedure .... `Esc`

Manage Links
(from Dependent Workbook)

1. Open or select dependent workbook

2. Click **Edit**, **Links** .... `Alt`+`E`,`K`

Excel lists all source workbooks for the dependent workbook.

To exit and return to dependent workbook:

Click [**Close**] .... [Esc]

To update values from source files:

a. Select source file(s) from **Source File** list.

b. Click [**Update Now**] .... [Alt]+[U]

To open source files:

a. Select source file(s) from **Source File** list.

b. Click [**Open**] .... [Alt]+[O]

To replace the source with another workbook:

a. Select source file to replace in **Source File** list.

b. Click [**Change Source...**] .... [Alt]+[C]

c. Select new source file in **File Name** list.

d. Click [**OK**] .... [↵]

Save Linked Workbooks

> *NOTE:* *Saving the source workbook(s) prior to saving the dependent workbook ensures that the workbook names in the external references are current.*

1. Select and save source workbook(s) supplying the linked references.

2. Select and save dependent workbook that received linked references.

Create One–Input Data Table

1. Enter initial value in input cell.

2. Enter series of substitution values in desired column or row.

3. Select cell to receive formula.

CREATE ONE–INPUT DATA TABLE (CONTINUED)

If substitution values are in column:
Select cell one position above and right of first substitution value.

If substitution values are in a row:
Select cell one position below and left of first substitution value.

4. Enter formula that refers to input cell.

5. Select data table range containing formula, substitution values, and cells where results will be displayed.

6. Click **D**ata, **T**able .... Alt +D, T

7. Specify reference to input cell.

If substitution values are in a row:
Select (in worksheet) or type reference to initial input cell in **Row Input Cell**.

If substitution values are in a column:
Select (in worksheet) or type reference (item A) to initial input cell in **Column Input Cell**.

8. Click OK .... ↵

Add Substitution Input Values to a Data Table

1. Type new substitution values in cells adjacent to table.

2. Select entire data table range *and* extend selection to include new cells.

3. Follow steps 6–8 above to create a one–input table, page 109.

Create a Lookup Table

Finds information located in a table:

- *VLOOKUP—compares values listed in a column.*
- *HLOOKUP—compares values listed in a row.*

1. Enter compare values in a column or row.
2. Enter data in cells adjacent to compare values.
3. Enter an initial compare value to find.
4. Select cell where result of lookup will appear.
5. Press = ... 🔳
6. Type function name, **VLOOKUP** or **HLOOKUP**.
7. Press ((open parenthesis) .... 🔳
8. Select (in worksheet) or type reference containing compare value to find.
9. Press , (comma) .... 🔳
10. Select (in worksheet) or type reference to entire lookup area.
11. Press , (comma) .... 🔳
12. Enter offset number representing the column offset (for VLOOKUP) or row offset (for HLOOKUP) in table where data is located.
13. Press) (close parenthesis) .... 🔳
14. Click [OK] .... 🔳

Create Array Formula

1. Enter values to be calculated by array formula in consecutive cells.

2. Select range of cells to receive array formula (the cells where results will appear).

3. Enter formula.
   NOTE: In the formula, be sure to specify entire range of cells containing values to calculate.

4. Press **Ctrl+Shift+Enter** .... `Ctrl`+`Shift`+`⏎`
   Excel adds braces ({ }) to formula and displays resulting values in each cell in array selection area).

Edit Array Formula

1. Double–click any result cell in array.

2. Edit formula as desired.

3. Press **Ctrl+Shift+Enter** .... `Ctrl`+`Shift`+`⏎`
   Excel changes all formulas in array.

Extend Array Formula to Include Additional Cells

1. Enter new values for array formula to calculate in cells adjacent to existing array data.

2. Select all cells in array and extend selection to include new cells where results will appear.

3. Double–click any result cell in array.

4. Edit formula as desired.
   NOTE: In the formula, be sure to include reference to cells containing new values to calculate.

5. Press **Ctrl+Shift+Enter** .... `Ctrl`+`Shift`+`⏎`

Find a Specific Solution to a Formula (Goal Seek)

1. Enter formula and dependent values.

2. Click **Tools**, **Goal Seek** .... Alt + T , G

3. Select (cell in worksheet) or type reference to cell containing formula in **Set cell**.

4. Type desired formula result value in **To value**.

5. Select (cell in worksheet) or type reference to cell containing value to change in **By changing cell**.

6. Click OK .... ⏎
   Excel displays status of goal seeking.

7. If desired, select **Goal Seek Status** options.

8. Click OK .... ⏎
   to replace value in worksheet with solution value.
   OR
   Click Cancel .... Esc
   to retain original values.

Use Solver to Find Best Answer

1. Enter formula and dependent values.

2. Click **Tools**, **Solver** .... Alt + T , V

   *NOTE: If **Solver** is not on the **Tools** menu, see **Install or Remove Add–In**, page 139.*

3. Select (in worksheet) or type reference to target cell in **Set Target Cell**.

   NOTE: Target cell typically contains a formula referring to cells that will change. If target cell is not a formula, it must also be included as a changing cell (step 4).

114   EXCEL

USE SOLVER TO FIND BEST ANSWER (CONTINUED)

4. Select (in worksheet) or type references to changing cells in **By Changing Cells**.

    *NOTES: Type commas between references to non–adjacent cells. Click the **Guess** button to have Solver propose changing cells.*

To solve for a specific value:

a. Select **Value of**.

b. Type target value in **Value of**.

To solve for a maximum or minimum target value:

(Requires you to set constraints)

Click **M**ax or Mi**n** .... Alt +M/N

To add constraints:

a. Click [**Add**] .... Alt +A

b. Click **Cell Reference** .... Alt +R , *reference* and type cell reference to apply constraint to.

c. Click **C**onstraint operator .... Alt +C

d. Click **C**onstraint .... Alt +C , *number* and specify constraint value.

NOTE: You can select (in worksheet) a reference in a cell containing the value or type a value or reference.

e. Click [**OK**] .... ↵

To change constraint:

a. Click **Subject to the Constraints** .... `Alt`+`U`
   and select constraint.

b. Click `Change...` .... `Alt`+`C`

c. Edit constraint elements.

d. Click `OK` .... `↵`

To delete constraint:

a. Click **Subject to the Constraints** .... `Alt`+`U`
   and select constraint.

b. Click `Delete` .... `Alt`+`D`

Create Scenario

Scenarios are named sets of input values that quickly show
different results in specified changing cells. There can be only
one set of changing cells in a worksheet.

1. Enter formula and initial values.

2. Click **Tools**, **Scenarios** .... `Alt`+`T`,`C`

   NOTE: If Scenarios is not on the Tools menu, see
   ***Install/Remove Add-In**, page 139.*

3. Click `Add` .... `Alt`+`A`

4. Click **Scenario Name** .... `Alt`+`N`, *scenario name*
   and type name for scenario.

5. Click **Changing Cells** .... `Alt`+`C`
   and type reference of changing cells.

   To edit comment:
   Edit text in **Comment** list.

To set scenario protection options:
Select/deselect **Protection** options.

6. Click [OK] .... ⏎

7. Type values in **each changing cell's** box.

To add scenario and create another scenario:

a. Click [OK] .... ⏎

b. Repeat steps 4–7, as needed.

8. Click [OK] .... ⏎

9. Click **Sçenarios** .... Alt + C
   and select scenario to show.

10. Click [Close]

11. If desired, repeat steps 9–10.

12. Click [Close]

PIVOT TABLES

Create Pivot Table

A pivot table is an interactive tool used to analyze information about worksheet data. For example, if you have a list containing information about expenses, a pivot table could evaluate the categories of these expenses, as shown in the illustration.

1. Click **Data**, **PivotTable** .... Alt + D , P

   PivotTable Wizard—Step 1 of 4

2. Select **Create PivotTable from data in** option.

3. Click [Next >] .... ⏎

    PivotTable Wizard—Step 2 of 4

4. If necessary, select (in worksheet) or type cell reference of data source in **Range**.

    *NOTE: You can click the **Browse** button, if data source is external. Then select a file containing data.*

5. Click [Next >] .... ⏎

    PivotTable Wizard—Step 3 of 4

6. Create pivot table layout.

    To add fields to pivot table:
    Drag field buttons onto a layout area.

    NOTE: You must include at least one field in the data area. You can drag more than one field button into a layout area, but it's best to limit the number of fields when starting out.

    To remove field from pivot table:
    Drag field button off the layout area.

    To move a field to another layout area:
    Drag field button onto desired layout area.

    To modify how the field is used:
    a   Double–click field button in layout area.

    b   Select **PivotTable Field** options.

7. Click [Next >] .... ⏎

    PivotTable Wizard—Step 4 of 4

CREATE PIVOT TABLE (CONTINUED)

8. Select (in worksheet) or type reference to upper–left destination of table in **PivotTable Starting Cell**.

   NOTE: If you leave this blank, Excel will create the pivot table on a new worksheet. Do not place the pivot table where it can overwrite existing data.

9. If desired, type name in **PivotTable Name**.

10. Select desired **PivotTable** options.

11. Click [**Finish**] .... `Alt`+`F`

Excel displays pivot table, and the Query and Pivot toolbar appears.

Modify Pivot Table.

1. Select cell in pivot table.

2. Click **PivotTable Wizard** .... `Alt`+`D`, `P`

3. Make changes to field layout.

4. Click [**Finish**] .... `Alt`+`F`

Update a Pivot Table

Updates a pivot table to show changes made to source data.

   NOTE: If rows or columns were removed or added to the source data range, you may have to follow the steps to modify a pivot table and change the reference to the source data.

1. Select any cell in pivot table.

2. Click **Refresh Data** .... `Alt`+`D`, `R`

Modify Pivot Table Field

Specifies how the pivot table will display or process the field data.

1. Double–click desired field button in pivot table.
2. Select **PivotTable Field** options.
3. Click ` OK ` .... ↵

Sort Pivot Table Data

1. Select any item in field to sort.

2. Click **D**ata, **S**ort .... `Alt`+`D`,`S`

   To change proposed sort by cell:

   Click **S**ort by and type reference to cell .. `Alt`+`S`

   To set sort order:

   Click **A**scending/**D**escending .... `Alt`+`A`/`D`

   To sort by values/alphabetically:

   Click **V**alues/**L**abels .... `Alt`+`V`/`L`

   NOTE: *To select Values, the **Sort by** reference (see above) must contain a value in the data area of the pivot table.*

   To select custom sort order (i.e., days or months):

   a. Click ` Options >> ` .... `Alt`+`O`

   b. Click **F**irst Key Sort Order .... `Alt`+`F`
      and select desired sort order.

   c. Click ` OK ` .... ↵

3. Click ` OK ` .... ↵

120

Sort Data

1. Select any cell in list, or range of cells to sort.

2. Click **D**ata, **S**ort............................ `Alt`+`D`,`S`

   To set first sort order:

   a. Click **S**ort By .... `Alt`+`S`
   and select field, column or row.

   b. Click **A**scending/**D**escending.... `Alt`+`A`/`D`

   To set second and third sort orders:

   Click **T**hen By.............................. `Alt`+`T`
   select field, column or row.

   To specify case sensitive sort order:

   a. Click `Options...` .... `Alt`+`O`

   b. Click **C**ase Sensitive...................... `Alt`+`C`

   c. Click `OK` .... `↵`

   To change orientation of sort (columns to rows):

   a. Click `Options...` .... `Alt`+`O`

   b. Click Sort **L**eft to Right .... `Alt`+`L`

   c. Click `OK` .... `↵`

   To include or exclude header row from sort:

   Click No Header Ro**w**/Header **R**ow ... `Alt`+`W`/`R`

3. Click `OK` .... `↵`

NOTES: *To sort by more than three columns, sort the list using the least important columns. Then, repeat the sort using the most important columns.*

When you sort rows that are part of an outline, Excel will keep outline families together. When you sort rows containing graphics, Excel will move the graphics with rows, if the graphics are set to move with the cell.

Perform Quick Sort

1. Select cell in list to sort by.

   NOTE: *Excel will apply setting made in a previous sort, if one was made.*

   OR
   Select range of cells to sort.
   NOTE: *The active cell in the range determines the column Excel will sort by.*

   OR
   Select item in pivot table field to sort by.

2. Click ⬆⬇ or ⬇⬆ .... **Alt**+**D**, **S**, **A** or **D**

Undo Sort

NOTE: *To successfully undo a sort, you must undo it immediately.*

Click **Edit**, **Undo Sort** .... **Alt**+**E**, **U**

Create/Edit Custom Lists

You can use a custom list to fill cells with a series and as a custom sort order.

1. Click **Tools**, **Options** .... **Alt**+**T**, **O**

CREATE OR EDIT CUSTOM LISTS (CONTINUED)

2. Click [Custom Lists] .... ⬅ ➡ ⬆ ⬇

    To create custom list:

    a. Click **Custom Lists** .... Alt + L
       and select **NEW LIST**.

    b. Click **List Entries** .... Alt + E
       and type list items.

    *NOTE: Items cannot begin with a number. Enter
    items in the order you want Excel to use
    when creating a series or sorting a list.*

    c. Click [**Add**] .... Alt + A

    To import custom list from worksheet:

    a. Click **Import List from Cells** .... Alt + I
       and type reference to cells containing list items.

    b. Click [**Import**] .... Alt + M

    To edit created custom list:

    a. Click **Custom Lists** .... Alt + L
       and select list to edit.

    b. Click **List Entries** .... Alt + E
       and edit items in list.

    To delete created custom list:

    a. Click **Custom Lists** .... Alt + L
       and select list to delete.

    b. Click [**Delete**] .... Alt + D

    c. Click [**OK**] .... ↵

3. Click [**OK**] .... ↵

LISTS

Excel automatically recognizes a labeled series of rows containing sets of data as a list. In a list, Excel treats rows as records and columns as fields. The field names are derived from the column labels.

Add Records to List (Data Form)

1. Select any cell in list.

2. Click **Data**, **Form** .... `Alt`+`D`,`O`

3. Click `New` .... `Alt`+`W`

4. Type data in each record field.

   NOTE: Press Tab to move to next field. Do not press Enter after typing data in field, unless you want to add another record.

   To add additional records:

   Repeat steps 3–4 for each record to add.

5. Click `Close` .... `Alt`+`L`

Delete Records from List (Data Form)

CAUTION: Deleted records cannot be restored.

1. Select any cell in list.

2. Click **Data**, **Form** .... `Alt`+`D`,`O`

3. Display record to delete.

4. Click `Delete` .... `Alt`+`D`

5. Click `OK` .... `↵`

   To delete additional records:

   Repeat steps 3–5 for each record to delete.

6. Click `Close` .... `Alt`+`L`

Excel deletes record in list, and moves records up to close the space left by the deletion.

124   EXCEL

Display/Edit Records (Data Form)

1. Select any cell in list.

2. Click **Data**, **Form**.....................【Alt】+【D】,【O】

   To view next/previous record:

   Click [**Find Next**].....................【Alt】+【N】/【P】

   or [**Find Prev**]

   To edit displayed record:

   Edit data in each record field.

   *NOTE: Do not press **Enter** after typing data in field.*

   To cancel changes made to current record:

   Click [**Restore**].............................【Alt】+【R】

   NOTE: You must restore before moving to another record.

3. Click [**Close**].............................【Alt】+【L】

Find Specific Records (Using a Data Form)

1. Select any cell in list.

2. Click **Data**, **Form**.....................【Alt】+【D】,【O】

3. Click [**Criteria**].............................【Alt】+【C】

4. Type a criterion for which to search in record field.

   *NOTE: Wildcard characters (? or *) may be used to stand for one (?) or more (*) characters in the position of the wildcard character. To find an actual ? or *, precede ? or * character with a tilde (~).*

FIND SPECIFIC RECORDS (CONTINUED)

EXAMPLES:

Type pau *in a text field to find records beginning with pau, such as* Paul *or* Paula.

Type >=1./1./89 *in a date field to find records containing dates on or after* 1./1./89.

Type (718) ???-???? *in a character field to find phone numbers that have a* 718 *area code.*

Type * Shaw *in a character field to find records that have any first name and* Shaw *as a last name.*

5. To add criteria to additional fields, repeat step 4..

6. Click **Find Next** / **Find Prev**   Alt + N / P

7. Repeat step 6 for each matching record to find.

   To obtain access to entire list:

   a. Click **Criteria** .... Alt + C

   b. Click **Clear** .... Alt + C

   c. Click **Form** .... Alt + F

8. Click **Close** .... Alt + L
   to return to worksheet.

Filter List Automatically

NOTE: You can use AutoFilter with one list in a worksheet at a time and the list must have column labels.

1. Click any cell in list.

2. Click **Data, Filter, AutoFilter**... Alt + D , F , F

126   EXCEL

FILTER LIST AUTOMATICALLY (CONTINUED)

Excel adds drop–down list arrows next to each column label.

3. Click ⬇ of label containing data to display.

4. Select desired item from list

   If Custom was selected:
   a. Select a column item in first.

   b. Select desired operator for item.

   To specify another criteria for column:
   a. Select **A**nd or **O**r.................. `Alt`+`A`/`O`

   b. Select column item in second.

   c. Select desired operator for item.

NOTE: *If you select criteria from more than one drop–down list, Excel will show only records meeting the criteria specified by both filters.*

End AutoFilter

Click **D**ata, **F**ilter AutoF**i**lter.......... `Alt`+`D`,`F`,`F`

Subtotal List Automatically

Creates subtotals for groups of data in specified columns, and a grand total at the bottom of the list. Excel automatically applies outlining to the resulting list.

   NOTE: *You can also do this to a filtered list.*

1. Sort column(s) in list to subtotal.

   NOTE: *List must contain labeled columns in its first row. Items to subtotal should be grouped together.*

2. Select any cell in list.

SUBTOTAL LIST AUTOMATICALLY (CONTINUED)

3. Select **Data, Subtotals** .... `Alt`+`D`,`B`

4. Select **At Each Change** .... `Alt`+`A`
   and select column label containing
   groups to subtotal.

5. Select **Use Function** .... `Alt`+`U`
   and select desired function.

6. Select **Add Subtotal** .... `Alt`+`D`
   and select column label(s) containing
   values to calculate.
   To replace or retain current subtotals:
   Select/deselect **Replace Current Subtotals**.
   To force page breaks between subtotaled groups:
   Select **Page Break Between Groups**.
   To place subtotals and grand totals above data:
   Deselect **Summary Below Data**.

7. Click [**OK**] .... `↵`

Outline Worksheet Automatically

NOTE: *In the data to outline, references in*
formulas must consistently point in one
direction (i.e., summary formulas in rows
must consistently refer to detail cells above
them).

1. Select single cell to outline entire worksheet.
   OR
   Select range of cells to outline

2. Click **Data, Group and** .... `Alt`+`D`,`G`,`A`
   Outline, Auto Outline.

Excel creates an outline and displays outline symbols to the left
of the row heading and/or above column headings.

Clear Entire Outline

1. Select and cell in outline.

2. Click **Data**, **Group and** .... `Alt`+`D`,`G`,`C`
   Outline, **Clear Outline**.

Remove Group from Outline

1. Select group in outline to remove.

2. Click **Data**, **Group and** .... `Alt`+`D`,`G`,`C`
   Outline, **Clear Outline**.

FORMAT

Change Column Widths

1. Point to right border of column heading

2. Drag ⬄ left or right.
   Excel displays width on left side of formula bar.

   To change several column widths:

   a. Select columns.

   NOTE: Click ⬜ to change all columns.

   b. Point to right border of selected column
      heading.

   c. Drag ⬄ left or right.
   Excel displays width on left side of formula bar.

   To set column width to fit the longest entry:
   Double–click right border of the column's heading.

Change Row Heights

1. Point to bottom border of row heading.

2. Drag ⬍ up or down.

Excel displays height on left side of formula bar.

To change several row heights:
a. Select rows.

b. Point to bottom border of selected row heading.

c. Drag ⊞ up or down.

To set row height to fit tallest entry:
Double–click bottom border of the row's heading.

To set row height to specific size:
a. Select any cell in row or rows to size.

b. Click **Format**, **Row**, **Height** ..... Alt + O , R , E

c. Enter number (0–4.09) in **Row Height**.

NOTE: Number represents height in points.

3. Click ▐ **OK** ▌ ....↵

Hide Column(s)

1. Point to right border of column heading.

   OR
   Select columns.

2. Drag ⊞ to column's left border.

Excel displays a bolded column heading border where a column is hidden.

OR
1. Select any cells in column(s) to hide

2. Click **Format**, **Column**, **Hide** .... Alt + O , C , H

Excel displays a bolded column heading border where a column is hidden.

Show Hidden Column(s)

1. Point just right of bolded column heading border

2. Drag ⊞ right.

OR
1. Select surrounding columns.

2. Click **Format**, **Column**, **Unhide** .... `Alt` + `O` , `C` , `U`

Hide Row(s)

1. Point to bottom border of row heading.

   OR
   Select rows.

2. Drag ⊞ up to row's top border.

Excel displays a bolded row heading border where a row is hidden.

OR
1. Select any cells in row(s) to hide.

2. Click **Format**, **Row**, **Hide** .... `Alt` + `O` , `R` , `H`

Excel displays a bolded row heading border where a row is hidden.

Show Hidden Rows

1. Point just below bolded row heading border.

2. Drag ⊞ down.

OR
1. Select surrounding rows.

2. Click **Format**, **Row**, **Unhide** ..... `Alt` + `O` , `R` , `U`

Align Data in Cells

1. Select cell(s) containing data to align.

—FROM FORMATTING TOOLBAR—

2. Click desired button.

left   center   right

OR

1. Select cell(s) containing data to align.
2. Click **Format**, **Cells**..................... `Alt`+`O`, `E`
3. Click `Alignment` .... `←` `→`
   and select desired horizontal/vertical option.
4. Click `OK` .... `↵`

Wrap Text in a Cell

1. Select cell(s) containing text to wrap.
2. Click **Format**, **Cells**..................... `Alt`+`O`, `E`
3. Click `Alignment` .... `←` `→`
4. Select **Wrap Text**................................. `Alt`+`W`
5. Click `OK` .... `↵`

Justify Text in Cells

1. Select cell(s) containing text to justify.
2. Click **Format**, **Cells**..................... `Alt`+`O`, `E`
3. Click `Alignment` .... `←` `→`
4. Select desired option(s).
5. Click `OK` .... `↵`

Center Data Across Columns

Centers data in left–most cells of a selection, across blank cells to the right. The centered data will remain in original cell(s).

1. Select cell(s) in one column containing data to center and adjacent blank cells to the right.

2. Click ⊞ .... **Alt**+**O**, **E**, **Alt**+**A**

Excel centers the data across selection of blank cells.

Change Font/Size/Color

1. Select cells or characters in cells.

2. Click **Format**, **Cells** .... **Alt**+**O**, **E**

3. Click [Font] .... **←** **→**

4. Make desired changes.

5. Click [OK] .... **↵**

Bold, Italicize, or Underline Text

1. Select cells or characters in cells.

—FROM FORMATTING TOOLBAR—

2. Click desired option.

Apply Custom Borders to Cells

1. Select cell(s).

2. Click **Format**, **Cells** .... **Alt**+**O**, **E**

3. Click [Border] .... **←** **→**

4. Select a style for border in **Style group**.

5. Select border to apply style to in **Border group**.

To remove border:
Click border again.

To change border color:
Select desired color in **Color**.

6. Repeat steps 4–5 for each border.

7. Click `OK` .... ↵

Apply Color to Cells

1. Select cell(s).

2. Click 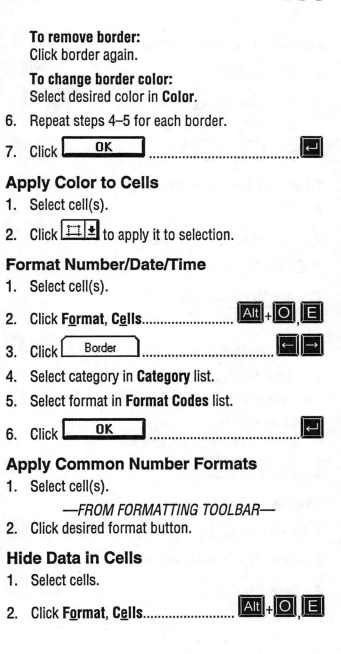 to apply it to selection.

Format Number/Date/Time

1. Select cell(s).

2. Click **Format**, **Cells**...................... Alt + O , E

3. Click `Border` .... ← →

4. Select category in **Category** list.

5. Select format in **Format Codes** list.

6. Click `OK` .... ↵

Apply Common Number Formats

1. Select cell(s).

—FROM FORMATTING TOOLBAR—

2. Click desired format button.

Hide Data in Cells

1. Select cells.

2. Click **Format**, **Cells**...................... Alt + O , E

HIDE DATA IN CELLS (CONTINUED)

3. Click [Number] .... ← →

4. Double–click in **Code** box .... ; ; ;
   to highlight existing code, and type

5. Click [OK] .... ↵

Clear All Formats Applied to Cells

1. Select cell(s).

2. Click **Edit**, **Clear**, **Formats** .... Alt + E , F

STYLES

Create Style by Example

1. Select cell containing desired formats.

2. Click **Format**, **Style**......................... Alt + O , S

3. Type **Style Name** in text box.

Excel displays the style's formats in Style Includes *box.*

To exclude format categories from style:
Deselect desired **Style Includes** options.

4. Click [OK] .... ↵

Create Style by Defining It

1. Click **Format**, **Style**......................... Alt + O , S

2. Type **Style Name** in text box.

3. Click [Modify...] .... Alt + M

4. Click tab of format category to include in style.

5. Select options for selected category.

6. Repeat steps 4–5 for each format category to include.

7. Click [**OK**] .... [↵]

To exclude format categories from style:
Deselect desired **Style Includes** options.

To define/apply style:
Click [**OK**] .... [↵]

To define style without applying it:

a. Click [**Add**] .... [Alt]+[A]

b. Click [**Close**]

Redefine Style by Example

1. Select cell containing desired formats.

2. Click **Format**, **Style** .... [Alt]+[O], [S]

3. Type **Style Name** in text box.

4. Click [**Add**] .... [Alt]+[A]

If Redefine prompt appears:

Click [**Yes**] .... [Alt]+[Y]

5. Click [**OK**] .... [↵]

Excel redefines style and updates cells formatted with style in worksheet.

Delete Style

1. Click **Format**, **Style**.........................$\boxed{Alt}$+$\boxed{O}$,$\boxed{S}$
2. Select desired **Style Name** to delete in text box.

   NOTE: Normal style cannot be deleted.

3. Click $\boxed{\underline{D}elete}$ ....$\boxed{Alt}$+$\boxed{D}$

4. Click $\boxed{OK}$ ....$\boxed{\hookleftarrow}$

AutoFormat Worksheet Data

1. Select any cell in data block to format.

   NOTE: The data block could be a list or a pivot table.

2. Click **Format**, **AutoFormat**..............$\boxed{Alt}$+$\boxed{O}$,$\boxed{A}$

3. Select desired format in **Table Format** list.

   To exclude parts of format:

   a. Click $\boxed{Options >>}$ ....$\boxed{Alt}$+$\boxed{O}$

   b. Deselect **Formats to Apply** options.

4. Click $\boxed{OK}$ ....$\boxed{\hookleftarrow}$

PRINTING

Set Page Options

1. Select **Page Setup** ....$\boxed{Alt}$+$\boxed{F}$,$\boxed{U}$

2. Click $\boxed{Page}$ ....$\boxed{\leftarrow}$$\boxed{\rightarrow}$

   NOTE: Available options will depend on the currently selected printer.

3. Select desired options.

4. Click **Page Setup** tab or command button.

EXCEL 137

Set Print Margins

1. Select **File**, **Page Setup**.............. `Alt`+`F`,`U`
2. Click [Margins] `←``→`
3. Select desired options.
4. Click [**OK**] `↵`

Set Header and Footer Options

1. Select **File**, **Page Setup**.............. `Alt`+`F`,`U`
2. Click [Header/Footer] `←``→`
3. Select desired options.
4. Click [**OK**] `↵`

Print

1. Select range(s) in worksheet(s) to print.
2. Click **File**, **Print** .... `Alt`+`F`,`P`
3. Select desired **Print What** options.
4. Click [**OK**] `↵`

WORKSPACE VIEWS

Split Worksheet into Panes

Provides simultaneous scrolling of up to four panes. You can freeze panes to prevent top, left or both panes from scrolling.

1. Point to horizontal or vertical split box on scroll bar.
2. Drag along scroll bar until split bar is in desired position.

Move Between Worksheet Panes

Click desired pane .... `F6`
until active cell is in desired pane.

Freeze/Unfreeze Panes on Split Worksheet
Locks top and/or left pane when scrolling.

Click **W**indow, **F**reeze Panes .... `Alt`+`W`,`F`

Freeze Titles

1. Select row below horizontal titles to freeze.

   OR
   Select column to right of vertical titles to freeze.

   OR
   Select cell below and to the right of horizontal and vertical titles to freeze.

2. Click **W**indow, **F**reeze Panes.......... `Alt`+`W`,`F`

Unfreeze Titles

Click **W**indow, Un**f**reeze Panes............. `Alt`+`W`,`F`

Set View Options
Sets display of many workspace and window elements.

1. Click **T**ools, **O**ptions .... `Alt`+`T`,`O`

2. Click [View] .... `←` `→`

3. Select desired options.

4. Click [OK] .... `↵`

Install/Remove Add–In

Add–ins are programs or functions you can add to Excel menus. They include Analysis ToolPak, AutoSave, Microsoft ODBC Function, Microsoft Query, Report Manager, Slide Show, Solver and View Manager.

1. Click **Tools**, **Add–Ins** .... `Alt`+`T`, `I`
2. Select/deselect add–ins in **Add–Ins Available** list.
3. Click `OK` .... `↵`

PROTECT WORKBOOK DATA

Protect Workbook

Prevents user from changing the way a workbook is arranged or displayed.

1. Select/open workbook to protect.
2. Click **Tools**, **Protection**,........... `Alt`+`T`, `P`, `W`
   Protect Workbook.

   To set password protection:
   Enter **Password (optional)** in text box.

   To protect workbook structure:
   Prevents sheets from being inserted, deleted, renamed, moved, hidden or unhidden.

   Select **Structure** .... `Alt`+`S`

   To protect workbook windows:
   Prevents windows from being closed, sized, moved, hidden or unhidden.

   Select **Windows** .... `Alt`+`W`
3. Click `OK` .... `↵`

PROTECT WORKBOOK (CONTINUED)

If password was entered:
a. Retype password.

b. Click ⟨ OK ⟩ .... ⌨

To unprotect workbook:
a. Select/open workbook to unprotect.

b. Click **Tools**, **Protection**, ... `Alt`+`T`,`P`,`W`
   Unprotect Workbook.

Protect Sheet

Prevents changes to locked cells, graphic objects, embedded charts in a worksheet or chart items in a chart sheet. By default, all cells and objects in a worksheet are locked.

1. Select sheet to protect.

2. Click **Tools**, **Protection**, ... `Alt`+`T`,`P`,`P`
   Protect Sheet.

   • Enter **Password (optional)** in text box to
     password protect sheet.

   • Select **Contents** .... `Alt`+`C`
     to protect cell contents and chart items.

   • Select **Objects** .... `Alt`+`O`
     to protect graphic objects.

   • Select **Scenarios** .... `Alt`+`S`
     to protect scenarios.

3. Click [OK   ] .... ⏎

   If password was entered:
   a. Retype password.

   b. Click [OK   ] .... ⏎

   To unprotect sheet:
   a. Select sheet to unprotect.

   b. Click **Tools**, **Protection**,...... [Alt]+[T],[P],[P]
      Unprotect Sheet.

   If sheet is password protected:
   a. Retype password.

   b. Click [OK   ] .... ⏎

Hide/Unhide Formulas

Hidden formulas will not appear on the formula bar. When you hide a formula, the setting takes effect when a sheet is protected.

1. If necessary, unprotect sheet.

2. Select cells containing formulas to hide.

3. Click **Format**, **Cells**...................... [Alt]+[O],[E]

4. Click [Protection] .... [←][→]

5. Select/deselect **Hidden**.......................... [Alt]+[I]

6. Click [OK   ] .... ⏎

7. Protect worksheet contents to enable hidden formulas.

GRAPHIC OBJECTS

Select Graphic Objects

To select one graphic object:
Click object.
To select multiple graphic objects:
Press **Shift** and click each object.

Create Text Box

1. Click 🖳

2. Position ✛ where corner of box will be.

   To create box without constraints:
   Drag box outline until desired size is obtained.
   To create square box:
   Press **Shift** and drag box outline until desired size
   is obtained.
   To create box and align it with gridlines:
   Press **Alt** and drag box outline until desired size is
   obtained.

3. Type desired text.

4. Click outside text box to return to normal
   operations.

Draw Graphic Objects

Draws objects such as rectangles and ellipses.

1. Click 🖳

   *NOTE: You can rest pointer on a button in the
   Drawing toolbar to show its name.*

2. Click desired drawing tool on Drawing toolbar.

3. Point to an area where a corner of object will begin.

4. Drag object's outline until desired size and shape is
   obtained.

Move Graphic Objects

1. Select graphic object(s) or chart item.

2. Point to border of any selected object.

3. Drag border outline to desired position.

    OR
    Press **Alt** and drag border outline to align object to gridlines.

Copy Graphic Objects

1. Select graphic object(s).

2. Point to border of any selected object.

3. Press **Ctrl** and drag border outline to desired position.

    OR
    Press **Ctrl+Alt** and drag border outline to align object to gridlines.

Size Graphic Objects

1. Select graphic object(s) or chart item.

2. Point to selection handle on side of border to size.

    NOTE: To size object proportionally, point to corner selection handle.

    To size object without constraints:
    Drag border outline until desired size is obtained.

    To size object and align to gridlines:
    Press **Alt** and drag border outline until desired size is obtained.

Delete Graphic Objects

1. Select graphic object(s).

2. Press **Delete** ....

Overlap Graphic Objects

1. Select graphic object(s).

2. Click ▣

3. Click **Bring To Front** ▣

    OR

    Click **Send To Back** ▣

Group/Ungroup Graphic Objects

1. Select graphic objects to group or ungroup.

2. Click ▣

3. Click **Group Objects** ▣

    OR

    Click **Ungroup Objects** ▣

Set Properties of Graphic Objects

Sets objects to move and size with underlying cells or chart.
Sets print property of object.

1. Select graphic object(s).

2. Click **Format, (Selected) Object**..... Alt + O , E

3. Click [Properties] .... ← →

4. Select desired **Object Positioning** option.

    To enable or disable printing of object:

    Select or deselect **Print Object** .... Alt + P

5. Click [OK] .... ↵

Insert Graphic File (Picture)

Inserts a graphic file into Excel. The supported file formats (such as .bmp and .pcx) will depend upon the filters selected when you installed Excel. You can add or remove these filters by running Excel Setup.

1. Select upper–left cell where graphic will be inserted.

2. Click **I**nsert, **P**icture .... `Alt`+`I`, `P`

3. Select graphic file.

   To preview picture before inserting it:

   Select **P**review Picture........................... `Alt`+`P`

4. Click `   OK   ` .... `↵`

CHART

Create Chart

1. Select cells containing data to plot.

2. a. Click **I**nsert, C**h**art .... `Alt`+`I`, `H`

   b. Click **On This Sheet** or **As New Sheet**, as desired.

   *NOTE: You can also click the **ChartWizard** button on the Standard toolbar to create an embedded chart on the worksheet.*

   If you clicked On This Sheet:
   Drag chart outline to desired size.

   *NOTE: To create a square chart, press **Shift** while dragging chart outline. To align chart with cell structure, press Alt while dragging chart outline.*

   ChartWizard—Step 1 of 5

CREATE CHART (CONTINUED)

3. If necessary, select (in worksheet) or type reference to cells to plot in **Range**.

4. Click [**Next >**] .... [↵]
   ChartWizard—Step 2 of 5

5. Click desired chart type.

6. Click [**Next >**] .... [↵]
   ChartWizard—Step 3 of 5

7. Click desired chart format.
   ChartWizard—Step 4 of 5

8. Select chart options.

   To change how to plot data series:
   Select **Rows** or **Columns**.

   Excel shows the result of your selections in a sample chart.

   To specify rows/columns to use for axis labels, legend text or chart title:
   Select number of rows/columns in **Use First**.

   NOTE: Options will depend on the chart type. To plot values in first row or column (not use them as labels) select 0 (zero).

9. Click [**Next >**] .... [↵]
   ChartWizard—Step 5 of 5

10. Select other chart options.

    NOTE: Available options will depend on the chart type.

11. Click [**Finish**] .... [Alt]+[F]

Enable Chart Editing
To edit embedded chart:
Double–click embedded chart.

The chart is surrounded by a thick border with handles, or if the entire chart was not displayed on the sheet, the chart appears in a window.

To edit chart sheet:
Select chart sheet.

Select Chart Items
You will select chart items prior to selecting commands to change the item in some way.

> *NOTE:*   *Excel marks the currently selected chart item with squares, and displays its name in the Name box.*

Double–click embedded chart.

To select next or previous class of chart items:

Press **arrow keys** .... ⬆️⬇️

To select next or previous subitem for selected chart class:

Press **arrow keys** .... ⬅️➡️

To select specific item with the mouse:
Click chart item.

To select data series with mouse:
Click any data marker in data series.

To select data marker with mouse:
a.   Click any data marker in data series.

b.   Click data marker in selected series

To select chart area with mouse:
Click any blank area outside plot area.

SELECT CHART ITEMS (CONTINUED)

To select plot area with mouse:
Click any blank area inside plot area.

To select legend or subitems with mouse:
NOTE: Legend subitems are the legend entry and key.

a. Click legend.

b. Click subitem in legend.

To deselect a selected chart item:
Press **Esc** .... Esc

Change Range of Data to Plot

1. Enable chart editing.

2. Click **ChartWizard** 📊

3. Select (in worksheet) or type reference to data to plot in **Range**.

4. Click [**Finish**] .... Alt + F

Change Orientation of Data Series to Rows or Columns

1. Enable chart editing.

2. Click **ChartWizard** 📊

3. Click [**Next >**] .... ↵

4. Select **Rows/Columns** .... Alt + R / C

5. Click [**OK**] .... ↵

Add Data to Chart Sheet

1. Select range of data to add to chart.

   NOTE: Include category or data series names.

2. Click **Edit, Copy** .... `Alt`+`E`,`C`

3. Select chart sheet.

4. Click **Edit, Paste** .... `Alt`+`E`,`P`

   If Paste Special dialog box appears:

   a. Select options appropriate to your chart and selection.

   b. Click ┃⎯⎯ OK ⎯⎯┃ .... `↵`

   *NOTE: If you make the wrong choices in the **Paste Special** dialog box, select **Undo** from the **Edit** menu.*

5. Press **Esc** to end copy .... `Esc`

Format Chart Type Group

   NOTE: By default, charts contain a single chart type group in which each data series is formatted in the same way. When you change a chart type for a data series, Excel creates a chart type group for that series. A chart with more than one chart group is often called a combination or overlay chart. When you plot data along a secondary axis, Excel also creates a chart type group for that series.

1. Enable chart editing.

2. a. Select **Format** .... `Alt`+`O`

150

FORMAT CHART TYPE GROUP (CONTINUED)

b. Click numbered chart type group at bottom of menu.

To plot group on primary or secondary axis:
(For charts containing more than one group)

a. Click [Axis] .... [←][→]

b. Select **Primary Axis** or **Secondary Axis**.

To select format options for chart type group:

a. Click [Options] .... [←][→]

b. Select **Format** options for group.

To change order of series in chart type group:

a. Click [Series Order] .... [←][→]

b. Select name of series in **Series Order** list.

c. Click [**Move Up**] / [**Move Down**]

To change subtype (style) for chart type group:

a. Click [Subtype] .... [←][→]

b. Click **Subtype** style.

3. Click [OK] .... [↵]

AutoFormat Chart
Applies a built-in or custom-made format to a chart.

1. Enable chart editing.

2. Click **Format**, **AutoFormat** .... [Alt]+[O],[A]

3. Click **Built-in** or **User-Defined** ..... [Alt]+[B]/[U]

4. Select desired chart type in **Galleries** list.

If applying built-in format:

Select desired autoformat in **Formats** list.

5. Click [OK] .... [↵]

Return Chart to Default Chart Type and Format

1. Enable chart editing.

2. Click **Default Chart** 🖼 on Chart toolbar.

Set Default Chart Options

> *NOTE: Available options will depend upon the chart type and where the chart is located (i.e., embedded or on a chart sheet).*

1. Enable chart editing.

2. Click **Tools**, **Options** .... `Alt`+`T`,`O`

3. Click [Chart] .... `←``→`

To set how empty cells are plotted in Line charts:
Select **Empty Cells Plotted as** option.

To set plotting of visible cells:

Select/deselect **Plot Visible Cells Only** .. `Alt`+`P`

To set chart sizing with window frame:

Select/deselect **Chart Sizes** .... `Alt`+`C`
with Window Frame.

To change the default chart:
Select chart type in **Default Chart Format**.

> *NOTE: Select **Built-in** to reset chart to original default type.*

To make current chart type the default chart:

a. Click [Use the Current Chart...] .... `Alt`+`U`

b. Type format name in **Format Name**.

c. Click [OK] .... `↵`

4. Click [OK] .... `↵`

Display/Hide Axes

1. Enable chart editing.

2. Click **Insert**, **Axes**.......................... Alt + I , X

3. Select/deselect **Category (X) Axis** .... Alt + C

   OR

   Select/deselect **Value (Y) Axis**.............. Alt + V

   If chart is 3–D:
   Select/deselect desired **Axis** options.

4. Click [OK] .... ↵

Insert Data Labels

Adds data labels to a data series or a specific data marker in a chart.

1. Enable chart editing.

2. Select data series or data marker to which label(s) will be added.

   OR
   Select chart or plot area to add labels to all data markers.

3. Click **Insert**, **Data Labels**............... Alt + I , D

4. Select **Data Labels** option.

   To display legend keys next to data labels:
   Select **Show Legend Key** next to Label.

5. Click [OK] .... ↵

   *NOTE: Data labels are linked to worksheet data
            and they can be edited in the worksheet,
            edited in the chart, formatted and moved.*

Insert Chart Title/Axes Labels

1. Enable chart editing.

2. Click **Insert**, **Titles** .... `Alt`+`I`, `T`

3. Select desired **Attach Text to** options.

   NOTE: Available options depend on chart type.

4. Click `OK` .... `↵`

   *NOTE: Chart titles and axes labels are not linked
   to worksheet data, and they can be edited
   in the chart, formatted and moved.*

Link Chart Text to Worksheet Data

*Chart text, such as legend entries, data labels and tick mark
labels are automatically linked to the data worksheet cells. You
can use this procedure to link other chart text (such as axis
labels, chart titles, text box text) to the contents of cells in a
worksheet.*

1. Enable chart editing.

2. Select chart item containing unlinked text.

3. Press = sign .... `=`

   Equal sign appears in formula bar.

4. Select (in worksheet) or type reference to cell
   containing text.

5. Press **Enter** .... `↵`

Insert Legend

1. Enable chart editing.

2. Click **Legend** 📇 .... `Alt`+`I`, `L`

   *NOTE: Legend entries are linked to worksheet
   data and they can be edited in the
   worksheet or in the chart. Legend, legend
   entries and keys can be formatted. You can
   also move and size the legend.*

Edit Legend Entry in Chart

1. Enable chart editing.
2. Double-click data series for legend to change.
3. Click [Name and Values] .... ⬅️ ➡️
4. Select reference (in worksheet) containing series name or type series name in **Name**.

   NOTE: If you type a name, the automatic link to the worksheet is ended.

5. Click [OK] .... ↵

Insert/Remove Gridlines

1. Enable chart editing.
2. Click **Horizontal Gridlines** 📊 .... Alt+ I ,G

   If you selected Gridlines from the menu:
   a. Select/deselect **Category (X/Y/Z) Axis** options.

   NOTE: Available options depend on chart type.

   b. Click [OK] .... ↵

Insert/Modify Error Bars

1. Enable chart editing.
2. Select data series to receive error bars.
3. Click **Insert, Error Bars** .... Alt+ I ,B
4. Select desired **Display** option.
5. Select desired **Error Amount** option.

If xy chart:

a. Select [Y Error Bars]

b. Select desired **Display** option.

c. Select desired **Error Amount** option.

6. Click [OK] .... [↵]

Insert Trendlines

1. Enable chart editing.

2. Select data series to plot trend for.

3. Click **I**nsert, T**r**endline .... [Alt]+[I],[R]

4. Click [Type] .... [←][→]

5. Select trend type in **Trend/Registration Type** list.

If Polynomial Order:
Type or select highest power for independent variable in **Order**.

If Moving Average Period:
Type or select number of periods for calculation in **Period**.

6. Click [OK] .... [↵]

Delete Chart Item

1. Enable chart editing.

2. Select chart item to delete.

3. Press **Delete** .... [Del]

NOTE: *If you delete the wrong items, select **Undo** from the **Edit** menu.*

Format Chart Text

1. Enable chart editing.

2. Double–click chart text or legend to format entire text.

   To change font:

   a. Click [Font] .... ⬅️➡️

   b. Select desired **Font** options.

   To change alignment and orientation of text:

   a. Click [Alignment] .... ⬅️➡️

   b. Select desired **Orientation** option.

3. Click [OK] .... ⏎

   NOTE: You can also format selected text or text in a selected chart item by clicking the desired format buttons on the Formatting toolbar.

Format Chart Numbers

1. Enable chart editing.

2. Double–click chart item containing values.

3. Click [Number] .... ⬅️➡️

4. Select desired category in **Category** list.

5. Select desired format in **Format Codes** list.

   To link edited data labels that are values to worksheet data:

   Select **Linked to Source** .... Alt+L

6. Click [OK] .... ⏎

Format Chart Items
1. Enable chart editing.
2. Double–click chart item to format.
3. Click [Patterns] .... ⬅️➡️
    NOTE: *Available options will depend on the chart
            item you double clicked.*
4. Select desired options.
5. Click [**OK**] ....↵

Size Chart's Plot Area/Legend
1. Enable chart editing.
2. Select plot area or legend.
    Handles appear on the item's border.
3. Point to handle on side of item to size.
4. Drag item outline in direction to size.

Move Chart Item
1. Enable chart editing.
2. Select chart item to move.
3. Drag chart item outline.

Position Legend in Chart
1. Enable chart editing.
2. Right–click legend.
3. Click **Format Legend** .... ⬆️⬇️
4. Click [Placement] ....➡️⬅️
5. Select desired **Type** option.
6. Click [**OK**] ....↵

OBJECT LINKING AND EMBEDDING

Create New Object and Embed It into a Worksheet

Inserts an object you create into another application so you can easily edit it from the source application.

1. Select cell where object will be inserted

2. Click **Insert**, **Object**........................ `Alt`+`I`,`O`

3. Click [Create New]

4. Select source application in **Object Type** list.

   To display inserted object as icon:

   Select **Display as Icon**.......................... `Alt`+`A`

   To change icon to be displayed:

   a. Click [**Change Icon...**] .... `Alt`+`I`

   b. Select **Icon** in list.

   *NOTE: You can click the **Browse** button to select another source file (i.e., MORICONS.DLL) for the icon.*

   c. If desired, edit **Caption**.

   d. Click [**OK**] .... `↵`

5. Click [**OK**] .... `↵`

6. Create object in application.

7. Double–click ▭ to close application.

8. Click [**Yes**] .... `Alt`+`Y`

Edit Object Embedded in Worksheet

> *NOTE:* *If object was created on another,*
> *connected computer, you can edit it only if*
> *the same application exists locally.*

1. Select object to edit.

2. Click **Edit**, **Object**, **Edit** .... Alt +E , O , E

3. Edit object in source application.

4. Double–click ⊟ to close application.

5. Click Yes .... Alt +Y

Embed Existing File into Worksheet

Inserts a file previously created in another application as an
object so you can easily edit the object from the source
application.

1. Select cell where object will be inserted.

2. Click **Insert**, **Object** .... Alt +I , O

3. Click ⌐ Create from File ⌐

4. Select file to embed in **File Name** list.

> *NOTE:* *To successfully embed the object, the*
> *application that created the file must*
> *support object linking and embedding (i.e.,*
> *Paintbrush or Sound Recorder).*

To display inserted object as icon:

Select **Display as Icon** .... Alt +A

160

To change icon to display:

a. Click `Change Icon...` .... `Alt`+`I`

b. Select desired **Icon** in list.

*NOTE: You can click the **Browse** button to select another source file (i.e., MORICONS.DLL) for the icon.*

c. If desired, edit **Caption**.

d. Click `OK` .... `↵`

5. Click `OK` .... `↵`

Delete Embedded or Linked Object in Worksheet

1. Select object to delete.

2. Press **Delete** .... `Del`

Link Object to Worksheet

1. Run or select application from which object originates.

   NOTE: Application must support object linking and embedding (i.e., Paintbrush or Sound Recorder).

2. Create or open file to link.

3. Save and name the file.

4. Select part of file to link.

5. Click **Edit**, **Copy** .... `Alt`+`E`,`C`

6. Run/select **Excel 5**.

7. Select cell where object will be inserted.

8. Click **Edit**, **Paste Special** .... `Alt`+`E`,`E`

9. Select **Paste Link** .... `Alt`+`L`

10. Select format to use in **As** list.

To display linked object as icon:
Select **Display as Icon**.

To change icon to display:

a. Click `Change Icon...` .... `Alt` + `I`
b. Select desired **Icon** in list.

*NOTE: You can click the **Browse** button to select
        another source file (i.e., MORICONS.DLL)
        for the icon.*

c. If desired, edit **Caption**.

d. Click `OK` .... `↵`

11. Click `OK` .... `↵`

Edit Linked Object in Worksheet

1. Select object to edit.

2. Click **Edit**, **Object** .... `Alt` + `E`, `O`

3. Edit object in source application.

4. Save the file.

5. Double-click `▬` to close application.

MACROS

Record Macro

1. If necessary, mark position for recording macro.

2. a. Click **Tools**, **Record Macro** .... `Alt` + `T`, `R`

    b. Click **Record New Macro** .... `R`

3. Type **Macro Name** in text box.

4. Type **Description** in text box.

5. Click `Options >>` .... `Alt` + `I`

6. Select desired options.

162

RECORD MACRO (CONTINUED)

7. Click [**OK**] .... ⏎
    A toolbar with a Stop Macro button appears.
    To set references to relative or absolute:

    a. Click **Tools**, **Record Macro** .... Alt + T , R
    b. Select/deselect **Use Relative References**.
8. Execute commands to record.
9. Click **Stop Macro** ▪ when done.
    *Excel adds a module or macro sheet to the end of the
    existing sheets in the workbook if you specified This
    Workbook, above.*

Play Back Macro

Press assigned shortcut key.
    OR

    a. Click **Tools**, **Macro** .... Alt + T , M
    b. Select macro to run.

    c. Click [**Run**] .... Alt + R
    OR

    Click **Tools** and select assigned macro name near
    bottom of menu.

Mark Position for Recording Macro

*Marks starting point in a module where a new macro will be
recorded or marks insertion point where recorded actions will
be inserted into an existing macro.*

1. Select module sheet containing macro.
2. Place insertion point in module where macro code
    will be inserted or new macro will begin.
3. a. Click **Tools**, **Record Macro** .... Alt + T , R

    b. Click **Mark Position for Recording** .... M

4. Select sheet and cell where recording will begin.

5. Record macro or record actions into existing macro *(see below)*.

Record Actions into Existing Macro

1. Mark *(see above)* position in existing macro where macro code will be inserted.

   NOTE: *If using MS Excel 4.0 macro language, insert cells in module to receive macro code. (You will need to edit the macro when done.)*

2. Click **Tools**, **Record** .... `Alt`+`T`, `R`, `E`
   Macro, Record at Mark.

3. Follow steps 6–8 for **Record Macro**.

ANNOTATE AND AUDIT WORKSHEET

Create Text Notes

1. Select cell to attach note to.

2. Click **Insert**, **Note** .... `Alt`+`I`, `T`

3. Type note in **Text Note** box.

   To add notes to other cells:

   a. Click ` Add ` .... `Alt`+`A`

   b. Select (in worksheet) or type cell reference for note in **Cell**.

   c. Type note in **Text Note** box.

   NOTE: *You can edit/delete existing text in* ***Text Note*** *box.*

CREATE TEXT NOTES (CONTINUED)

    d. Repeat steps a–c, as needed.

4. Click [**OK**] .... [↵]

View/Edit Text Notes

1. Select cell containing note.

> *NOTE: Cells with notes have a small square in upper–right corner.*

2. Click **Insert**, **Note** .... [Alt]+[I],[T]

3. View/edit note in **Text Note** box.

To view/edit additional notes:

    a Select cell containing note in **Notes in Sheet** list.

    b View or edit note in **Text Note** box.

    c Repeat steps a–b, as needed.

4. Click [**OK**] .... [↵]

Delete Notes

1. Select cell(s) containing note(s).

2. Click **Edit**, **Clear**, **Notes** .... [Alt]+[E],[A],[N]

BACKGROUND
Add Background Items
Add Art

1. Select **V**iew, **M**aster .... `Alt`+`V`,`M`

2. Select **Slide Master** .... `S`

3. Create, paste or insert graphic object on master.

4. Select art object and drag to desired position.

5. Size and edit art object, as desired.

6. Click 🖳 on status bar to return to presentation.

Add Text

1. Select **V**iew, **M**aster .... `Alt`+`V`,`M`

2. Select **Slide Master** .... `S`

3. Click **A** on tool palette.

4. Position ⊥ where text should begin and click.

5. Type desired text...................................... ...... *text*

6. Edit and enhance text, as desired.

7. Click 🖳 on status bar to return to presentation.

Add Date/Time

1. Select **V**iew, **M**aster...................... `Alt`+`V`,`M`

2. Select **Slide Master** .... `S`

3. Click **A** on tool palette.

4. Position ⊥ where date/time appears and click.

ADD DATE/TIME (CONTINUED)

5. Type // to position date ....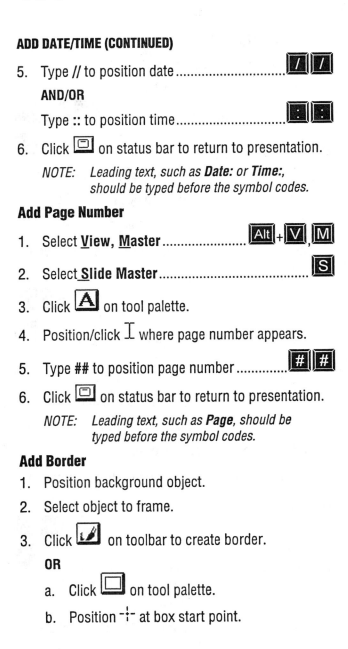

AND/OR

Type :: to position time ....

6. Click ▢ on status bar to return to presentation.

> *NOTE:*   *Leading text, such as **Date:** or **Time:**,
> should be typed before the symbol codes.*

Add Page Number

1. Select <u>V</u>iew, <u>M</u>aster .... Alt + V , M

2. Select <u>Sl</u>ide Master .... S

3. Click A on tool palette.

4. Position/click ⌶ where page number appears.

5. Type ## to position page number .... # #

6. Click ▢ on status bar to return to presentation.

> *NOTE:*   *Leading text, such as **Page**, should be
> typed before the symbol codes.*

Add Border

1. Position background object.

2. Select object to frame.

3. Click ▨ on toolbar to create border.

OR

a. Click ▢ on tool palette.

b. Position ⊹ at box start point.

   c. Click and drag ┄┼┄ to opposite corner (end point), making sure entire object is enclosed within box.

4. Edit lines/fill, as desired.

Copy Background

1. Open presentation containing background to copy.

2. Display Slide Master view.

3. Delete items not wanted for new slide presentation.

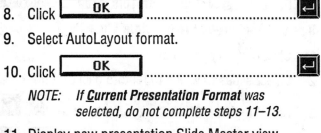

4. Select **Edit Select All** .... `Alt`+`E`, `A`

5. Click 🗐 .... `Ctrl`+`C`

6. Click 🗋 .... `Ctrl`+`N`

7. Select desired format options.

    *NOTE: If **Pick a Look Wizard** or **Template** is selected, you need to select the desired layout before continuing.*

8. Click �again [**OK**] .... `↵`

9. Select AutoLayout format.

10. Click [**OK**] .... `↵`

    *NOTE: If **Current Presentation Format** was selected, do not complete steps 11–13.*

11. Display new presentation Slide Master view.

12. Delete items not wanted on new master.

13. Click 🗐 .... `Ctrl`+`V`

168 POWERPOINT

Remove Background
Remove Background from One Slide
1. Display desired slide.
2. Select **Format, Slide Background...** `Alt`+`F`,`G`
3. Deselect **Display Objects on This Slide** .... `Alt`+`O`

Remove Background from Multiple Slides
1. Click `⊞` on status bar.
2. Select slides from which to remove background.
3. Select **Format Slide Background...** `Alt`+`O`,`G`
4. Deselect **Display Objects on These Slides**. `Alt`+`O`

Restore Background
Restore Background to One Slide
1. Display desired slide.
2. Select **Format, Slide Background...** `Alt`+`F`,`G`
3. Select **Display Objects on This Slide** .... `Alt`+`O`

Restore Background to Multiple Slides
1. Click `⊞` on status bar.
2. Select slides to which to restore background.
3. Select **Format, Slide Background...** `Alt`+`F`,`G`
4. Select **Display Objects on These Slides** `Alt`+`O`

POWERPOINT   169

Shade Background

1. Make slide.
2. Select **Format, Slide Background** .. `Alt`+`O`, `G`
3. Select desired shade pattern/style.
4. Select `Apply` or `Apply To All` to apply.

BULLETS
Add/Delete Bullets

Since the default setting includes bullets, creating a new slide automatically places bullets in front of each text line.

Add Bullet

1. Position `I` in line to contain bullet.
2. Click `▤` to place default bullet.

Remove Bullet from Specific Slide

1. Position cursor in line to remove bullet.
2. Deselect `▤` on toolbar.

Remove Bullet from Slide Master

1. Select **View, Master** .... `Alt`+`V`, `M`
2. Select **Slide Master** ....`S`
3. Position cursor at master body level from which to remove bullet.
4. Click `▤` on toolbar.
5. Repeat steps 3-4 until bullet is removed from all desired levels.
6. Click `▢` on status bar to return to presentation.

Bullet Font/Format
Select Bullet Font/Format

> *NOTE: To change bullet font on all slides, access the slide master before completing the following instructions. To change the bullet font for an individual slide within a presentation, return to the slide.*

1. Position cursor on line containing bullet font to change.

2. Select **Format, Bullet**..................... Alt +O , B

3. Select desired font set from text box.

> *NOTE: The font sets available depend on the printer and font sets installed on your machine.*

4. Select desired bullet character.

5. Select **Use a Bullet** check box.

6. Click OK .... ↵

Change Bullet Size

1. Position cursor on bullet to change.

2. Select **Format Bullet**..................... Alt +O , B

3. Click **Size** scroll box in upper right corner.

4. Enter desired percentage .... *number*

5. Click OK .... ↵

Format Bullet Indent

> *NOTE: The ruler requires the use of the mouse; it is not accessible from the keyboard.*

Move Indent

1. Position cursor in text level containing indent to adjust.

2. Select **V**iew, **R**uler ....

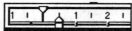

3. Drag markers to adjust bullet/text indent positions.

    NOTE: One set of markers appears on the ruler for each level of bulleted item appearing on the slide (up to a maximum of 5). The marker at the top controls the bullet position only. The marker at the bottom controls the position of the text following the bullet. When the square portion of the bottom marker is moved, the bullet and text are relocated, and the distance between the bullet and the text remains unchanged. When the triangular portion of the bottom marker is moved, only the text is repositioned.

4. Select **V**iew **R**uler to hide ruler ......

Remove Indent

1. Position cursor in text level containing indent to remove.

2. Select **V**iew **R**uler to display ruler..

3. Drag lower marker until it is aligned with upper marker.

    NOTE: One set of markers appears on the ruler for each level of bulleted item appearing on the slide (up to a maximum of 5).

REMOVE INDENT (CONTINUED)

The marker at the top controls the bullet position only.

The marker at the bottom controls the position of the text following the bullet. When the square portion of the bottom marker is moved, the bullet and text are relocated, and the distance between the bullet and the text remains unchanged.

When the triangular portion of the bottom marker is moved, only the text is repositioned.

4. Select **View Ruler** to hide ruler....... Alt + V , R

Turn Bullets On/Off

Turn Bullets On

1. Position cursor in text level to contain bullet.

2. Click ▤ on toolbar.

3. Click [OK] .... ↵

Turn Bullet Off

1. Position cursor in text level containing bullet to turn off.

2. Click ▤ on toolbar.

3. Click [OK]

Periods

1. Select **Format** .... Alt + O

2. Select text to end in periods.

3. Select **Periods** .... R

4. Select **Add Periods** or **Remove Periods** ...... A or R

5. Click [OK] .... ↵

CHARTS/GRAPHS
Start Graph
*There are three ways to enter the Graph feature: from the AutoLayout window, the **Insert Graph** button on the toolbar, or the menus.*

Start Graph Using Toolbar
1. Display slide to contain graph.
   OR
   Create new slide.
2. Click ▦ on toolbar.
   NOTE: A default graph is placed on the slide, and the datasheet window is presented.

Start Graph Using AutoLayout
1. Click ⌈ New Slide... ⌉ on status bar.
2. Select an AutoLayout slide that includes a graph placeholder.

Enter Data
1. Display datasheet window.
2. Position cursor in desired cell.
3. Type data.. *data*
4. Press **Enter**...⏎
5. Repeat steps 2–4 until all data is entered.

Enter Series in Rows
1. Click ▦ on toolbar .... Alt + D , R
2. Type data series names down column A.
3. Type category names across row one.
4. Type data across each row.

Enter Series in Columns

1. Click ⊞ on toolbar.
2. Type data series names across row one.
3. Type category names down column A.
4. Type data down each column.

Copy Data

1. Select cells containing data to copy.
2. Click 📋 .... Ctrl + C
3. Position cursor in first cell to receive data.
4. Click 📋 .... Ctrl + V
5. Repeat steps 3–4 until data is placed in as many cells as needed.

Clear Data

*Clearing or deleting data does not place it on the clipboard. The action can be reversed using the **Undo** feature. The clear command allows you to clear data, format or both.*

1. Select cell(s) containing data to clear.
2. Press **Delete** .... Del

Insert Row(s)/Column(s)

1. Display datasheet.
2. Click row/column frame button(s) (i.e. 1, 2, 3 or A, B, C) for new row(s)/column(s).
3. Select **I**nsert, C**e**lls .... Alt + I , E

If you selected the row or column frame button(s), new row(s) or column(s) are inserted at the selected row or column position(s).

If you selected a single cell or range of cell(s):

a. Select **Entire Row** or **Entire Column**, as desired.

b. Click [OK   ] ....[↵]

Delete Row(s)/Column(s)

1. Display datasheet.
2. Select frame button(s) for column(s)/row(s) to delete.
3. Select **Edit, Delete** .... [Alt]+[E],[D]

If you selected a single cell or range of cell(s):

a. Select **Entire Row** or **Entire Column**.

b. Click [OK   ]

Change Column Width

1. Display datasheet.
2. Position mouse pointer on border to right of frame button for column to widen.

    Mouse pointer changes to a ✚

3. Click and drag border to desired width.

OR

1. Display datasheet.
2. Select any cell in column to widen.
3. Select **Format Column Width** .... [Alt]+[O],[W]
4. Enter desired **Column, Width** ....*number*

    OR

    Click [**Best Fit**] to have PowerPoint set column width based on number of characters in longest data entry.

5. Click [OK   ] ....[↵]

Reset Column Width

1. Display datasheet.
2. Select any cell in column to reset.
3. Select **F**ormat, **C**olumn **W**idth .... `Alt`+`O`,`W`
4. Select **U**se **S**tandard **Width** check box option.
5. Click ⬛ **OK** .... `↵`

Format Numeric Data

1. Select cell(s) to format.
2. Select **F**ormat, **N**umber .... `Alt`+`O`,`N`
3. Select desired **C**ategory to access list of Format Codes.
4. Select desired format code in **F**ormat Codes.
5. Click ⬛ **OK** .... `↵`

Format Cell Text

1. Display datasheet.
2. Select **F**ormat, **F**ont .... `Alt`+`O`,`F`
3. Select desired option(s).
4. Click ⬛ **OK** .... `↵`

Format Tick–Mark Labels

1. Display datasheet.
2. Position cursor in cell A2 to make it active.
3. Select **F**ormat, **N**umber .... `Alt`+`O`,`N`
4. Select desired **C**ategory to access list of Format Codes.
5. Select format code in **F**ormat Codes list which contains symbol desired on axis (such as $).
6. Click ⬛ **OK** .... `↵`

Work with Graphs
Activate Graph

Click 🖻 to deactivate .... Alt + V , D

OR

Click graph object visible behind datasheet.

Select Graph Type

1. Click 📊± on toolbar.

2. Select desired chart type.

3. Click [OK] if necessary.

Select Graph Series

Select desired graph bar, point, etc.

Move Legend

1. Select legend object; drag to new location.

Remove/Insert Legend

Click 🗒 .... Alt + I , L

> *NOTE:* *Inserting a legend places it in the default*
> *location. It may be moved to a new*
> *location.*

Recolor Graph

1. Display graph.

2. Double–click desired item to change color.

   OR

   Select F**o**rmat, S**e**lected Series ..... Alt + O , E

   > *NOTE:* ***Series*** *may be replaced by **Chart Area**,*
   > ***Walls, Axis, Plot Area** or **Legend**,*
   > *depending on the selected object.*

3. Select desired color.

Change Data Value from Chart

NOTE: Only available for 2D charts and XY scatter charts.

1. Display graph.

2. Select data item to change.

3. Click size handle or data point and drag to new value.

   NOTE: As you drag the size handle, the value in the datasheet changes to reflect new value.

Rotate Chart

NOTE: Only available for 3D charts.

Click graph frame and drag to new angle.

OR

1. Display graph.

2. Select **Format**, **3-D view** .... Alt + O , 3

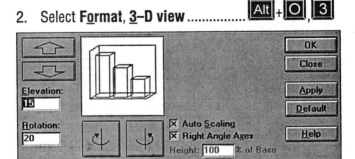

3. Click ⬓ to rotate left or ⬔ to rotate right.

   OR
   Enter desired **Rotation** number.

4. Enter **Elevation** number in text box, if desired.

   OR
   Click ⬆ or ⬇

POWERPOINT

179

ROTATE CHART (CONTINUED)

5. Select desired option(s).

6. Click **Apply** to view effects of changes.

7. Click **OK** .... ⏎

Create Combination Chart

> *NOTE: You cannot combine 3D and 2D chart
> types in the same graph.*

1. Display graph.

2. Select data element to change series type.

3. Select **Format**, **Chart Type** .... `Alt`+`O`, `C`

4. Select **Selected Series**.................................. `S`

Delete Data Series

1. Display graph.

2. Select data series to delete.

3. Press **Delete** .... `Del`

   OR

   Select **Edit**, **Clear**, **Series** .... `Alt`+`E`, `A`, `S`

Change Value Axis Scale

1. Display graph.

2. Double–click value axis.

3. Click **Scale** tab.

4. Enter value in corresponding box.

5. Select desired option(s).

6. Click **OK** .... ⏎

Insert Titles

1. Select **I**nsert, **T**itles .... `Alt`+`I`,`T`
2. Select desired title option to **Attach Text to.**
3. Click `OK` .... `↵`
4. Type new title... *title*
5. Select title.
6. Select **F**ormat .... `Alt`+`O`, Selected *object* Title

   NOTE: The selected title type appears as the
   object *in the step above.*
7. Select desired text formatting options.
8. Click `OK` .... `↵`

Insert Data Labels

1. Select **I**nsert, **D**ata Labels .... `Alt`+`I`,`D`
2. Select desired **Data Labels** option.

   *NOTE: **Percent** is displayed only for pie charts.*

Edit Data Label

1. Select data label to edit.
2. Position cursor in text.
3. Type new text .... *text*
4. Press **Enter**.. `↵`

Format Options

1. Double–click item to change.
2. Select tab for item to change.
3. Select desired options.
4. Click `OK` .... `↵`

COLOR

*PowerPoint 4.0 has a new **Drawing+** toolbar which offers several arranging buttons for quicker access and ease of use. It is used throughout this section.*

Apply Color to Objects

Color Lines

1. Select object containing lines to color.
2. Click [icon] on toolbar.
3. Select desired color.
4. Click [OK] twice, if necessary.

Color Fill

1. Select object to fill.
2. Click [icon] on toolbar.
3. Select desired color.
4. Select desired color on color palette.

   *NOTE: When a color is selected from the **Other Color** dialog box, it is placed on the palette so it is available for future use.*

5. Click [OK] twice, if necessary.

Color Text

1. Select text to color.
2. Click [icon] on toolbar.
3. Select desired text color.
4. Click [OK] if necessary.

Color Shadow

1. Select object containing shadow to color.

    NOTE: If the selected object is not shadowed, this procedure has no effect.

2. Click 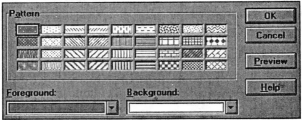 on toolbar.
3. Select desired shadow color.
5. Click [**OK**   ] if necessary.

Apply Patterned Fill to Objects

Add Pattern Design

1. Select object containing fill to pattern.
2. Click ▨ **Drawing+** toolbar.
3. Click **Pattern**.

4. Select desired pattern on pattern palette.
5. Click [**OK**   ] twice, if necessary.

Color Pattern Fill

1. Select object containing pattern to color.
2. Click ▨ on **Drawing+** toolbar.
3. Click **Pattern**.
4. Click ⊡ beside **Foreground** drop–down box.
5. Select desired color.
6. Click ⊡ beside **Background** drop–down box.
7. Select desired color.
8. Click [**OK**   ]

Apply Shaded Fill to Objects
Add Shaded Fill

1. Select filled object to shade.

2. Click 🖼 on **Drawing+** toolbar.

3. Click **Shaded**.

4. Select desired **Shade Styles** option.

   *NOTE: The best way to get an idea of the different shade styles is to select each and view the results in the **Variants** box.*

5. Select desired design in **Variants** sample box.

6. Click ⬆ beside **Color** drop–down box.

   To adjust shading brightness:

   Drag **Dark: Light** scroll box, as desired.

7. Click ⬛ **OK** ....⏎

DEFAULTS

Change Startup Defaults

1. Select **Tools**, **Options** .... Alt + T , O

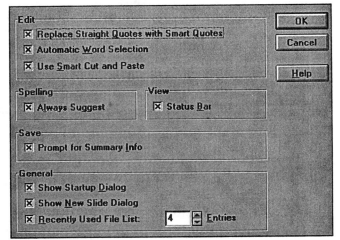

2. Select desired option(s).

Create Default Presentation

1. Open or create presentation to use as default.

2. Select **File**, **Save As** .... Alt + F , A

3. Type in **File Name** box .... *default.ppt*

4. Click [OK] .... ⏎

Default Fonts

1. Open presentation containing font to change or create new presentation.

> *NOTE:* *To change the font in the default presentation, select **Blank Presentation** in opening PowerPoint window.*

2. Display slide master.
3. Position cursor in desired text.
4. Select **Tools, Replace Fonts** .... `Alt`+`T`, `F`
5. Select or type font to replace in **Replace** box.
6. Select or type font to replace with in **With** box.
7. Click **Replace** drop–down list box.
8. Click [**Close**] .... `Alt`+`C`

DRAW

*The **draw tools** appear on one of the tool palettes, on the left side of the slide screen. While the same basic procedure is used to draw with most of the tools, each has its own default settings.*

Draw Object

Draw Shapes

1. Select desired draw tool.
2. Position -¦- at point where shape should start.
3. Click/drag to point where shape should end.
4. Release mouse button.

    NOTE: Objects do not have to be perfectly sized; they may be resized after being drawn.

Draw Arrowhead

1. Select line for arrowhead or draw new line.
2. Click 🗗 on **Drawing+** toolbar.
3. Select desired arrowhead style.
4. Click [**OK**] if necessary.

GRAPHICS/PICTURES

Clip Art

*The first time you open the **Clip Art Gallery**, you are asked which categories of clip art you want to add to the active Clip Art Gallery. Once a category is added, it remains available to you. If you add all categories, the prompt does not reappear. If you add selected categories, you are asked if you want to add additional categories each time you open the Clip Art Gallery.*

Add Clip Art

1. Click [🖾] .... [Alt]+[I],[C]

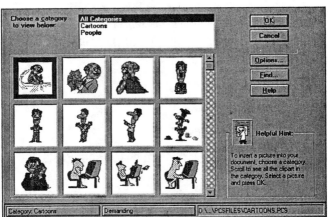

2. Select category from **Choose a <u>c</u>ategory to view below** list to present group of images.

3. Double–click desired image.

4. Adjust, move or size image as desired.

Find Clip Art

1. Click [🖾] .... [Alt]+[I],[C]

2. Click [**Find...**] .... [Alt]+[F]

PowerPoint 187

FIND CLIP ART (CONTINUED)

3. Position cursor in desired text box to search for image.
4. Type text for image .... *text*
5. Click **OK** ....⏎

Pictures

Insert Picture

1. Display slide to contain picture.
2. Select **Insert**, **Picture** .... **Alt**+**I**,**P**
3. Specify path containing desired picture.
4. Select desired filename in **File Name** list box.

*NOTE: To restrict filenames presented to certain file types, specify files to list in **List Files of Type** drop-down box.*

5. Click **OK** ....⏎

Save Slide as Picture

Saves slides as graphic images as Windows metafile.

1. Click ⬜ or ⬛ on status bar.
2. Display/select slide to save.
3. Select **File**, **Save As** .... **Alt**+**F**,**A**
4. Select **Windows Metafile** or **Scrapbook (Pictures)** in **Save File as Type** drop-down list box.
5. Type **File Name** in text box.

NOTE: A file extension of .wmf is automatically added to the filename of Windows files.

6. Specify path, if desired.
7. Click **OK** ....⏎

Crop Picture/Graphic

CAUTION: Do not confuse this feature with resizing the picture.

1. Display slide containing graphic/picture.

2. Select graphic/picture to crop.

3. Select **Tools, Crop Picture**.............. ![Alt]+![T],![P]

The mouse pointer takes shape of ⊹ .

4. Position ⊹ on selected graphic/picture handle.

5. Drag mouse across picture until cropped as desired.

6. Click neutral area of slide to exit Crop mode.

GUIDES

Helps with alignment of text and other objects. Available only in Slide view and Notes Pages view.

Display/Remove Guides

When guides are displayed, they are positioned at the 0.00 point (center), both horizontally and vertically.

Select **View, Guides**..................................

Move Guides

1. Position pointer on horizontal or vertical guide.

2. Click and drag guide to new location.

3. Release mouse button.

NOTE: When the horizontal guide is moved down the slide or the vertical guide is moved left, the position number is sometimes preceded by a – to indicate a negative x or y position.

IMPORT/EXPORT

Import Text

*PowerPoint imports text into outline form from Rich Text
Formats (RTF) and plain text formats from most word
processing applications. PowerPoint picks up the outline
structure from the styles used in a file. If no styles are used, the
paragraph indents or tabs are used to create the outline.
Imported outlines containing more than five text levels will be
adjusted so levels six and higher will be treated as level five
text.*

Import Outline

1. Click 📂 .... `Ctrl`+`O`
2. Select **Outlines** in **List Files of Type** box.
3. Select path containing outline text, if needed.
4. Select file in **File Name** text box.
5. Click [**OK**] .... `↵`

   NOTE: *A slide is generally prepared for each
   heading in imported text. Once the text is
   imported, it may be moved and arranged,
   as desired.*

Insert Outline in Presentation

1. Display slide where outline will start.
2. Select **Insert**, **Slides from Outline** . `Alt`+`I`, `L`
3. Select path containing outline text, if needed.
4. Select file type in **List Files of Type**.
5. Select file in **File Name**.
6. Click [**OK**] .... `↵`

Drag and Drop

When PowerPoint is part of the Microsoft Office Suite of products, it can work directly between Microsoft Excel 5.0, Microsoft Word 6.0, Access and Microsoft Mail and Schedule+. By selecting information within these applications, text can be dragged and dropped directly into your presentation.

1. Open PowerPoint target presentation.
2. Display target slide.
3. Open source application and file.
4. Select information to place in PowerPoint slide.
5. Tile windows on screen so both are accessible.
6. Drag selected information onto PowerPoint slide.

MASTERS AND TEMPLATES

Masters hold the format for text and background items appearing on every slide in a presentation. When a master is followed, the entire format of a presentation may be changed by simply changing the format on the slide master. You may, however, remove the master items and change the color scheme for selected slides or for sections of a presentation to create special effects. Changes made to the format of individual slides do not affect the master. There is a separate master for each key component of your presentation: notes, handouts and outlines. The procedures for formatting and working with all masters are the same.

Templates incorporate master layouts and add color and design to create a unified or consistent look to slides in a presentation. When applied to an active presentation, all slides within the presentation are formatted according to the template masters. Individual slides may not contain different templates. There are over 100 professionally designed templates available in PowerPoint 4.0.

Display Master

> NOTE: A master must be displayed to edit it in any way. This applies to all master types.

1. Select **View**, **Master** .... [Alt]+[V], [M]
2. Select **Slide Master** .... [S]
3. Select desired **Master** option.

> NOTE: Changes made to outline, handouts or notes masters do not affect other slides or the slide master.

Add Text Box as Background

> NOTE: This procedure applies to all master types.

1. Display master.
2. Click [A] on toolbar.
3. Position ⊥ outside text placeholder.
4. Type text .... *text*
5. Enhance by drawing box, etc., as desired.

Add Time, Date, Number as Background

> NOTE: This procedure applies to all master types.

1. Display master.
2. Click [A] on tool palette.
3. Position ⊥ outside text placeholder where item is to appear.
4. Type ## at position for page number .... [#][#]
   OR
   Type :: at position for time .... [:][:]
   OR
   Type // at position for date .... [/][/]

> NOTE: Page numbers, times and dates only appear on slides during the slide show or on printed slides, handouts or note pages.

Set Page Number

NOTE: This procedure applies to all master types.

1. Select **File**, **Slide Setup**................. `Alt`+`F`,`U`

2. Type number in **Number Slides From:**

3. Click `   OK   ` .... `↵`

Slide Master

Four formatting options appear on the slide master:

- *The Master Title format for slide titles*
- *The Master Body format for slide text*
- *Background items (such as page numbers)*
- *Master Color Scheme*

Format Slide Master Title

You may move the master title, resize the title box or font, change or enhance the font, and/or change the title alignment. Standard procedures for formatting text and moving and resizing objects should be used.

Format Slide Master Body

You may move the master body text, resize the body box or font, change or enhance the font, and/or change the body alignment. You may also wish to change the bullet style for different body text levels

Vary Slide Master Features on Slide(s)

Varies the look of selected slide(s) within a presentation. Individual items may be reformatted without affecting the Slide master or other slides.

1. Display slide to change.

2. Modify font, background and/or color scheme.

Remove Slide Master Background Items from Slide

1. Display slide from which to remove background items.

2. Select **Format, Slide Background** ...... [Alt]+[O],[G]

3. Select **Display Objects on This Slide** to deselect objects from slide master.

4. Click [**Apply**] or [**Apply To All**]

Reapply Slide Master Format

1. Display slide to which to reapply master.

2. Select **Format, Slide Layout** .... [Alt]+[O],[O]

3. Click [**Reapply**] .... [Alt]+[A]

Reapply Slide Master Color Scheme

1. Display slide to which to reapply color scheme.

2. Select **Format, Slide Color Scheme** .... [Alt]+[O],[C]

3. Click [**Follow Master**] .... [Alt]+[F]

4. Click [**Apply**] or [**Apply To All**]

Notes Master

Three formatting options appear on the notes master:
- *Slide Image*
- *Master Body*
- *Background*

Format Notes Master Slide Image

Lets you move, size and/or change the border of the slide image. Text and other features may not be edited. Procedures for working with images are the same as working with other objects.

1. Select **View, Master** .... [Alt]+[V],[M]

2. Select **Notes Master** ....[N]

3. Click **Slide Image**.

To move:
Drag image to new location.

To size:
Drag side or corner resize handle of image.

To change border:
a. Click ▤ .... Alt + O , L
b. Click desired line style.

Outline Master

Contains only a placeholder for the outline. Background items may be added following the procedure for other masters.

Handout Master

Determines how the handouts will appear based on the number of slides printed per page. Background items are added as described earlier.

Templates

Changes a slide so its attributes differ from the slide master. You cannot, however, apply a template to an individual slide. Whenever you apply a template, the entire presentation is affected. Slides following different templates may be inserted into blank presentations.

Template Types

Over 100 professionally designed templates are available in three different output formats:

- *Black and White Overheads: bwovrhd folder*
- *Color Overheads: clrovrhd folder*
- *Slide Show: sldshow folder*

Apply Template

1. Open presentation, or create new one.
2. Click `Template...` .... `Alt`+`O`, `P`
   on status bar.
3. Click folder containing desired template type in
   Directories list box.
4. Select desired template in **File Name** text box.
   NOTE: As a template is selected, a preview of the
   format is presented in the lower right-hand
   corner of the window.
5. Click `Apply` .... `Alt`+`A`
   NOTE: All slides in the active presentation are
   formatted using the selected template.

Vary Templates Within Presentation

Once a template is applied to a presentation, all slides follow
the template. This procedure creates a presentation using file
slides to which different templates have been applied.

1. Prepare presentations and save individually for
   each template used.
2. Create new, blank presentation.
3. Select **Insert, Slides from File** ...... `Alt`+`I`, `F`
4. Select one file containing slides with desired
   template.
5. Press **Ctrl** .... `Ctrl`
   and select additional files containing
   slides with desired templates.
6. Click `OK` .... `↵`
7. Click `⊞` on status bar.
8. Delete unwanted slides.
9. Save presentation using new filename.

AutoLayout

AutoLayout provides a number of preformatted slide layouts to make slide preparation more efficient. It may, at times, be necessary to vary the objects contained in one of the AutoLayout formats. This can be done by changing the placeholder for an existing AutoLayout format.

1. Open presentation, or create new one.
2. Select placeholder to replace.
3. Click desired toolbar button for object to use.

   NOTE: If supplemental application is opened,
   select File, Exit and Return Object to
   PowerPoint, *responding Yes if prompted;*
   or follow other appropriate procedures.

NOTES AND HANDOUTS

Create Notes

1. Click 🖳 on status bar................... `Alt`+`V`,`N`
2. Position cursor in placeholder, at bottom of page.
3. Type note text ....*text*

Add Lines to Notes

1. Prepare presentation, or open existing one.
2. Click 🖳 on status bar.

   NOTE: To place lines on all note pages in presentation,
   display notes master before proceeding.

3. Click 📝 on toolbar.
4. Draw line across notes area from margin to margin.
5. Select **Edit, Duplicate**.............................`Ctrl`+`D`
6. Position duplicate line below original.
7. Select **Edit, Duplicate Again**...................`Ctrl`+`D`
8. Repeat step above until notes section contains desired number of lines.

Handout Notes

1. Select **View**, **Master** .... Alt + V , M

2. Select **Handout Master** .... D

3. Click A on toolbar.

4. Position ⊥ outside image placeholders.

5. Type desired text .... *text*

OBJECTS

Select Object

> *NOTE:* To work with an object in any way, it must
> first be selected.

Select One Object

1. Click ▨ on toolbar.

2. Position pointer on desired object.

3. Click mouse button.

Select Multiple Objects

1. Click ▨ on tool palette.

2. Position pointer near leftmost and uppermost
   desired object.

3. Drag selection rectangle around objects until all are
   included in faint outline.

Deselect One Object from Those Selected

1. Follow procedures above to select objects.

2. Press and hold **Shift** .... Shift
   and click object to deselect.

Select All Objects

Select **E**dit, **S**elect **A**ll .... Ctrl + A

To deselect all objects:

Press **Esc** .... Esc

Group/Ungroup Objects

*Objects can be grouped so they can be moved, sized, etc.,
together. They may also be ungrouped so individual
components which make up the object can be edited. Grouped
objects which are made up of a number of subgrouped objects
are ungrouped level by level.*

Show Drawing+Tool Palette

1. Position pointer on any toolbar or tool palette.

2. Click *right* mouse button to display quick list of
   toolbars.

3. Display **Drawing+** toolbar.

Group Objects

1. Select objects to group.

2. Click ⊞ on **Drawing+** toolbar ...... Alt + D , G

3. Repeat steps 1–2 until all subgroups are
   regrouped.

Ungroup Objects

1. Select object to ungroup.

2. Click ⊞ on **Drawing+** toolbar ...... Alt + D , U

3. Repeat steps 1–2 until object subgroups are
   ungrouped, as needed.

POWERPOINT

Regroup Objects

1. Select **D**raw, **R**egroup .... [Alt]+[D],[R]
2. Repeat step 1 until all objects are regrouped.

Enhance Objects
Add/Remove Line

1. Select object to add or delete line.
2. Click [icon] .... [Alt]+[O],[L],[L]
3. Select **No Line** to remove line from object.
   OR
   Click desired line color to add line.
4. Click [OK] if necessary.

Add/Remove Fill

1. Select object to fill.
   NOTE: It will be necessary to double–click to select a freeform drawing.
2. Click [icon] .... [Alt]+[O],[L],[F]
3. Select **No Fill** to remove fill from object.
   OR
   Select desired fill color to add fill.
4. Click [OK] if necessary.

Add Shadow

1. Select object(s) to shadow.
2. Click [icon] .... [Alt]+[O],[H]
3. Select desired option(s).
   *NOTE: If the **Shadow** window appears, click the drop–down arrow beside the **Color** text box to display the options.*
4. Click [OK] if necessary.

Emboss Object

1. Select object to emboss.

2. Click 🖼 .... Alt +O,H,C

3. Click **Embossed**.

4. Click ⎸ OK ⎹ if necessary.

Modify Objects

Size/Resize Objects

1. Select object(s) to size.

2. Use one of the following techniques to resize:
   - Click and drag a handle until desired size is achieved.
   - **Shift** and drag handle to maintain proportions (aspect ratio) of object and avoid distortion.
   - **Ctrl** and drag handle to resize object from its center.
   - **Ctrl+Shift** and drag handle to resize horizontally, vertically or diagonally from the center outward.

To return object to original size after resizing:

Press **Shift** and double–click ... Shift , *double–click* any handle.

To return object to original aspect ratio (proportion):

Double–click any handle.

The picture remains sized but will be proportionally defined by reducing the distorting extension.

Scale Objects

1. Select object to scale.
2. Select **D**raw, Sca**l**e .... [Alt]+[D],[L]
3. Enter **S**cale To percentage number in text box.
4. Select **R**elative to Original Picture Size check box option, if desired.

   NOTE: ***Relative to Original Picture Size** option applies only to pictures imported from other applications.*

5. Click [OK] .... [↵]

Change Object Shape

1. Select object to change.
2. Click and drag adjustment handle.

   OR

   Click [icon] .... [Alt]+[D],[C]
3. Select desired shape.

Change Arc Shape

1. Select arc to change, or draw new arc.
2. Double–click arc .... [Alt]+[E],[O]
3. Drag handle until desired size and curve of the arc is obtained.
4. Release mouse button.

Edit Freeform Shape

1. Double–click object to edit .... [Alt]+[E],[O]
2. Position -¦- on any vertex (handle).
3. Hold mouse button and drag vertex to new position.
4. Release mouse button.

Add Vertex Point

1. Double–click object to edit.............. 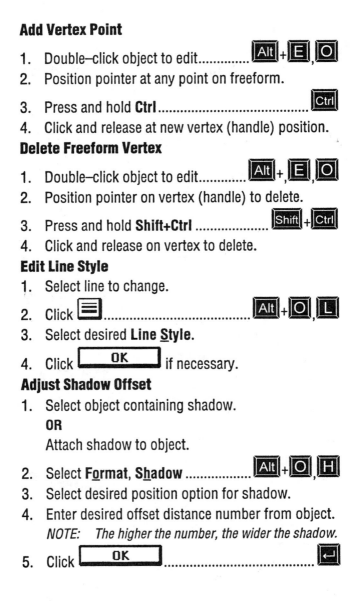 Alt + E , O
2. Position pointer at any point on freeform.

3. Press and hold **Ctrl** .... Ctrl
4. Click and release at new vertex (handle) position.

Delete Freeform Vertex

1. Double–click object to edit............ Alt + , E , O
2. Position pointer on vertex (handle) to delete.

3. Press and hold **Shift+Ctrl** .... Shift + Ctrl
4. Click and release on vertex to delete.

Edit Line Style

1. Select line to change.

2. Click ≣ .... Alt + O , L
3. Select desired **Line Style**.

4. Click   OK   if necessary.

Adjust Shadow Offset

1. Select object containing shadow.
   OR
   Attach shadow to object.

2. Select **Format, Shadow** .... Alt + O , H
3. Select desired position option for shadow.

4. Enter desired offset distance number from object.
   NOTE: The higher the number, the wider the shadow.

5. Click   OK   .... ↵

Flip Object

1. Select object to flip.

2. Click ⬜ or ⬜ on **Drawing+** toolbar.

Rotate Object Left/Right

1. Select object to rotate.

2. Click ⬜ or ⬜ on **Drawing+** toolbar.

Rotate Freely

1. Select object to rotate.

2. Click ⬜

3. Position modified mouse pointer on any handle and drag to desired angle.

   NOTE: *To control the rotation and limit it to 45 degree angles, hold **Shift** down while you drag the handle. Holding the **Ctrl** key while dragging a handle causes the opposite handle to act as the anchor point.*

Align Objects

1. Select objects to align.

2. Select **D**raw, **A**lign .... ⬜Alt⬜+⬜D⬜,⬜A⬜

3. Select desired alignment option.

Stack/Layer Objects

Bring Forward One Layer

1. Select object to bring forward.

2. Click ⬜

3. Repeat step 2 until object appears on desired level.

Send Backward One Layer

1. Select object to send back.
2. Click
3. Repeat step 2 until object appears on desired level.

Bring Object to Front

1. Select object to position on top.

   NOTE: It may be necessary to send a larger object back to gain access to the object on the bottom.

2. Select **Draw, Bring to Front** .... Alt + D , T

Send Object to Bottom

1. Select object to position on bottom.
2. Select **Draw, Send to Back** .... Alt + D , K

Cycle Through Objects

Press **Tab** .... Tab
to move from object to object.

OR

Press **Shift+Tab** .... Shift + Tab
to move backwards from object to object.

Hide Objects

1. Select object to hide.
2. Click
3. Select **Background**.

The object with the same color as that of the background.

4. Click
5. Click **No Line**.

Find Hidden Object

Select **E**dit, Select **A**ll .... Ctrl + A

> NOTE: Outlines of all objects are revealed with
> handles on the edges. **Select All** is a
> toggle switch which must be turned off to
> remove the outlines of the objects.

ORGANIZATIONAL CHARTS

Create Organization Chart

1. Click 🖳 on status bar.

2. Click ⊞ on toolbar.

Add Text

1. Select box to contain text.

2. Type text, press **Enter** ....*text,* Enter
   to advance to next line.

3. Press **Esc** to exit box .... Esc

   OR
   Click another box.

Create Chart Title

1. Open presentation and Organization Chart.

2. Click and drag across text to select **Chart Title**.

3. Type new title.

   > NOTE: If no chart title is added, the words **Chart
   > Title** are not on your slide.

Select Box(es)

Select Using Mouse

- **Single object** ....*click*
- **Multiple objects** .... Shift +*click*
- **Group** ....*double-click*

NOTE: *Mouse pointer should be a selection arrow.*
           A group is the collection of all boxes on the
           same level.

- **Branch** .... *click top box,* Ctrl + B

NOTE: *This approach selects the active box and*
           all branches of the box.

- **Box to left** .... ←
- **Box to right** .... →
- **Box above** .... ↑
- **Box below** .... ↓

Edit Organization Chart

Double-click organization chart on slide to activate
Organization Chart program.

Add/Delete Boxes

Add Boxes

1. Click desired box tool to add:

   - Subordinate: ⎍
   - ⬜⊦:Co-worker
   - Co-worker: ⊣⬜
   - Manager: ⊓
   - Assistant: ⬜⊣

2. Select chart box to attach new box.

Add Multiple Boxes

1. Click desired box tool once for each box to add.

2. Select chart box to attach new boxes.

Add Box Between Manager and Subordinate(s)

1. Select first box to assign to new manager.

2. Press **Shift** .... Shift
   and select additional boxes.

3. Press **Ctrl**, click Manager: ⊓ .... Ctrl
   to group selected boxes under new manager.

Delete Box

1. Select box to delete.

2. Press **Backspace/ Delete**.......... Backspace / Del

Move Boxes

CAUTION: Save your chart before moving boxes.

Move Box to New Manager/Subordinate

1. Select box to move.

The mouse pointer must remain a ⬚ rather than an I

2. Drag box using pointer, over new supervisor'sbox.

The box changes shapes and arrows display placement as you move the box over the new supervisor allowing you to select proper placement.

3. When desired placement is indicated, release mouse button.

Move Complete Chart

Click and drag top level box up or down.

NOTE: The mouse pointer must remain a pointing arrow to move chart.

Rearrange Layout

1. Select supervisor for level to rearrange.

2. Select **Styles**... Alt + S

3. Select desired arrangement for subordinates.

Save Chart

1. Click ⊞ on toolbar.

2. Select **File**, **Save Copy As**, *filename* .... Ctrl + S

3. Change path, if desired.

4. Click [OK] .... ↵

   CAUTION: Save your chart frequently, especially
   before rearranging, moving or editing it.

Place Chart in Slide

1. Open chart, or create new one.

   —IN ORGANIZATION CHART APPLICATION WINDOW—

2. Select **File**, **Update Presentation** ... Alt + F , U
   to place chart in presentation
   without exiting Organization Chart application.

   OR

   Select **Exit and Return to Presentation** .. Alt + F , X
   to place chart in presentation
   and exit Organization Chart application.

Open Chart

1. Click ⊞

2. Select **File**, **Open** .... Ctrl + O

3. Select/type desired **File Name** in text box.

4. Click [OK] .... ↵

Chart Options
—IN MS ORGANIZATION CHART WINDOW—
1. Prepare chart containing desired settings.
2. Select **Edit, Options**....................... `Alt`+`E`, `N`
3. Select desired option(s) to preset for new charts.
4. Click `OK` .... `↵`

PRESENTATIONS
Create Presentation
Starting PowerPoint allows you to create a new presentation. A new presentation may be created from any view within PowerPoint. Once a presentation is created, slides may be added and text and other objects may be imported or created directly on the slides.

1. Click `□` .... `Ctrl`+`N`
2. Make selections in **New Presentation** dialog box, as desired.
3. Click `OK` .... `↵`

Add Slides
1. Select desired view.................. **View**, *desired view* from status bar.
2. Position pointer where new slide will appear.
3. Click `New Slide...` on status bar.
4. Select format for new slide.
   NOTE: If slide format option has been discontinued, skip step 4.
5. Click `OK` .... `↵`

   NOTE: The new slide will become the active slide in the presentation and other slides will be moved to appear after the new slide.

Cut/Delete Slide

Delete Slide

The delete key may be used only in the Slide Sorter and Outline views.

1. Click ⊞ or ☰ on status bar.

2. Select slide to delete.

3. Press **Delete**.. Del

> *NOTE:*   *Deleting the slide does not place it on the clipboard for later use. If a slide is deleted in error, the action can be reversed.*

Cut Slide

Places the slide on the clipboard from which it may then be pasted into another presentation, another location within the current presentation or into another application entirely.

The Cut command is only available using the Slide Sorter view and the Outline view.

1. Click ⊞ or ☰ on status bar.

2. Select slide to cut.

3. Click ✂ .... Ctrl + X

> *NOTE:*   *If a slide is cut in error, the action can be reversed.*

Move/Reorder Slides

Slides may be moved or reordered easily from either the Outline view or the Slide Sorter view.

Move/Reorder in Slide Sorter View

1. Open presentation, or create new one.

2. Click ⊞ on status bar................... Alt + V , D

3. Select slide to move.

4. Drag slide to new position.

As you drag, the mouse pointer becomes a ⇕. Position the arrow between the two slides, before the first slide or after the last slide to select new slide position.

5. Release mouse button.

6. Repeat steps 3-5 until all slides are positioned as desired.

Move Around Presentation

Select Slide in Slide Sorter View

1. Open presentation, or create new one.

2. Click ▦ on status bar.................. `Alt`+`V`,`D`

3. Select desired slide.

4. Double-click [1] |▭ to move to Slide view.

    OR

    Click ▭ .... `Alt`+`V`,`S`
    on status bar.

Advance Slides in Slide View

1. Open presentation, or create new one.

2. Click ▭ on status bar.................. `Alt`+`V`,`S`

3. Click ▼ or ▲ to advance/backup.

    NOTE: *You cannot advance past the last slide or back up past the first slide. The slides themselves do not form a continuous loop. You may, however, set up a slide show to show in a continuous loop.*

Presentation Effects

Add Transition

1. Open presentation, or create new one.

2. Display slide to carry transition.

3. Click ⊞ on status bar.

4. Click ▣ .... Alt + T , T

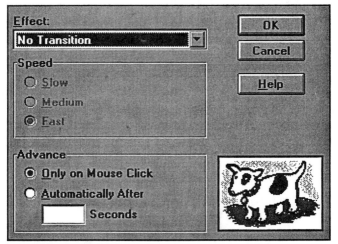

5. Select **Effect** from drop-down list.

6. Select desired speed for effect option.

7. Select advance method.

8. Click [OK] .... ↵

> NOTES: In Slide Sorter view, ▣ appears below
> each slide containing a transition.
>
> Transitions without a speed specification
> may be selected from the **Transition** text
> box on the toolbar of the Slide Sorter view.

Set Advance Method

1. Open presentation, or create new one.

2. Display slide to carry advance.

3. Click ⊞ on status bar.

4. Click 🔲 .... `Alt`+`T`,`T`

5. Select desired **Advance** option(s).

> NOTE: In Slide Sorter view, the number of
> seconds (converted to minutes and
> seconds if over 60 seconds) will be
> displayed below each slide to which timing
> is added.

PRINT AND OUTPUT

*PowerPoint 4.0 allows you to set up slide formats and print all
components of your presentation using the same basic
procedure. In addition, you can print to a file for outputting to a
service bureau from which you can obtain 35mm slides.*

Set Slide Format

1. Open presentation, or create new one.

2. Select **File, Slide Setup** .... `Alt`+`F`,`U`

3. Select desired options.

SET SLIDE FORMAT (CONTINUED)

> *NOTE:*   *The paper sizes for each of these selections will vary according to active or selected printer.*

4. Click [**OK**] .... [↵]

Print Presentation

Print slides, notes, handouts and outlines using same procedure on standard or special paper and transparencies.

1. Open presentation, or create new one.

2. Click [🖨] .... [Ctrl]+[P]

3. Select desired option in **Print What** text box.

> *NOTE:*   *If Outline view is selected, PowerPoint will print amount of text currently displayed on outline—titles or full text. Outlines will print using the standard 6.5" typing line, but text size is determined by zoom control in effect; i.e., 24 point text prints as 12 point with 50% zoom control.*

4. Select item to print.

5. Set number of **Copies** in text box.

6. Select slides to print.

7. Select desired check box options.

> *NOTE:*   *To send to service bureau for 35mm slides, a special driver is required. Contact service bureau for further information.*

8. Click [**OK**] .... [↵]

SLIDES

Add/Create Slide

When PowerPoint is started, a new presentation is created containing one slide. Additional slides may be created from any view, but slides may be edited only in Outline view and Slide view.

Add/Create Slide in Slide View

1. Click 🔲 .... `Alt`+`V`, `O`

2. Complete active slide.

3. Click `New Slide...` on status bar.

4. Select desired layout from **New Slide** dialog box.

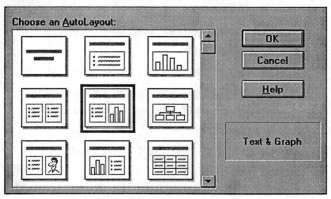

5. Click `OK` .... `↵`

Cut/Delete Slide

1. Click 🔡 or 🗒 on status bar.

2. Select slide to remove.

3. Click ✂ .... `Ctrl`+`X`

Add Text to Slide

Text may be added to slides in either the Slide view or the Outline view. Text added in Notes Pages view do not appear on slides.

Add Text in Slide View

1. Click ▣ on status bar.
2. Display slide to contain text.
3. Click title placeholder.

   NOTE: The title placeholder is the box containing the instruction to click to add title.

4. Type first slide title ....*title*

5. Press **Tab** ....
   to add body text to first slide.

   OR

   Click body text placeholder to add body text.

   NOTE: The body text placeholder is the outlined box containing the instructions to click to add text.

6. Type body text of first line or bullet item.

7. Press **Enter**..

   To add subsidiary level (demote):

   Press **Tab** ....

   *NOTE: Additional subsidiary levels (up to 5) may be added, as needed. To return to a previous level (promote) for a bulleted item, press **Shift+Tab**. Additional text at the same level are automatically accessed unless text is promoted or demoted.*

8. Repeat steps 6–7 until all text for first slide is complete.

9. Click New Slide... on status bar .... Ctrl + ⏎

10. Repeat steps 3–9 until all slides are complete.

Add/Delete Objects

Objects include items such as drawings, pictures, text, etc., you want to include on slides. The basic procedure for adding objects to slides is the same for objects that are already composed.

> NOTE: *Graphics and other objects do not appear in the Outline view. Slides containing graphics are indicated with a graphic slide icon.*

Add Graphic/Picture

1. Display slide to contain graphic.

2. Select **I**nsert, **P**icture .... Alt + I , P

3. Select drive and directory name containing graphic.

4. Select file type and graphic filename.

5. Click OK .... ⏎

6. Select options on Graphic Import window, if necessary.

7. Click OK

8. Click/drag to position object, as desired.

9. Click/drag handle to resize object.

Add Clip Art

1. Display slide to contain clip art.
2. Click 🖼 .... Alt + I , C
3. Select desired category containing clip art to place.
4. Select desired clip art picture to place.
5. Click [OK] .... ↵
6. Size and place clip art, as desired.

Add Drawing

1. Display slide to contain drawing.
2. Select desired tool palette draw tool.
3. Position ⁻ᵢ⁻ on slide at draw shape starting point.
4. Click and drag ⁻ᵢ⁻ until draw shape is complete.
5. Move, size and enhance drawing, as desired.

Delete Objects

1. Display slide containing graphic.
2. Select object to delete.
3. Click ✂ .... Ctrl + X

Copy Slide

Copy Entire Slide

1. Click 🎛 or 🗒 on status bar.
2. Select slide icon to copy.
3. Click 📋 .... Ctrl + C
4. Position cursor to paste slide.
5. Click 📋 .... Ctrl + V
6. Repeat 2–5 until all slides have been copied.

PowerPoint

Copy Selected Text/Objects
Slide view should be used when copying text or objects.

1. Display slide containing object in Slide view.
2. Select object/text to copy.
3. Click 📋 .... `Ctrl`+`C`
4. Position cursor on slide to contain object.
5. Click 📋 .... `Ctrl`+`V`

Build Slide

*A **build slide** uses a bullet chart and presents it one bullet item at a time. A build slide may be created using the Slide Sorter, Outline or Slide view. The build button is available, however, only in the Slide Sorter view.*

Create Build Slide

1. Click ▦ or ▤ or ▢ on status bar.
2. Select slide to use as a build slide.

   OR
   Click ▦ on toolbar in Slide Sorter view.
3. Select **T**ools, **B**uild .... `Alt`+`T`, `B`
4. Select **B**uild Body Text .... `B`
5. Select **D**im Previous Points or **E**ffect, as desired.
6. Click ⟨ OK ⟩ .... `↵`

Remove Build Feature

1. Click ⊞ or ⊟ or ⊡ on status bar.

2. Select build slide to remove Build feature.

    OR
    Click ⊞ from toolbar in Slide Sorter view.

3. Select **T**ools, **B**uild .... Alt + T , B

4. Select **B**uild Body Text to deselect .... B

5. Click [OK] .... ↵

Format Slides

1. Open presentation containing slides to format.

2. Select **F**ile, **S**lide Set**u**p .... Alt + F , U

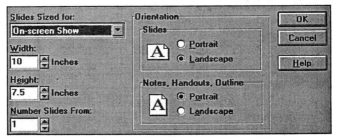

4. Select desired **S**lides Sized for option.

5. Select **P**ortrait or **L**andscape orientation, as desired.

6. Enter page **W**idth (inches) .... *number*

7. Enter page **H**eight (inches) .... *number*

8. Enter starting page number in **N**umber Slides From text box.

9. Click [OK] .... ↵

SLIDE SHOWS

Run Slide Show

Presentations may be shown using PowerPoint defaults without adding effects.

Show Complete Presentation

1. Open presentation, or create new one.

2. Select **Automatic** or **Manual Advance**, as desired.

3. Click 🖳 on status bar.

4. Press **Enter** to advance slides .... ⏎

   OR
   Click mouse button to advance slides.

Show Selected Slides

1. Open presentation, or create new one.

2. Select **View**, **Slide Show** .... **Alt**+**V**, **W**

3. Enter slide numbers ....*number*
   to show in **From** and **To** text boxes.

4. Select desired **Advance** method option.

5. Click 🖳 on status bar.

Run Continuously

1. Open presentation, or create new one.

2. Select **View**, **Slide Show** .... **Alt**+**V**, **W**

3. Enter slide numbers ....*number*
   to show in **From** and **To** text boxes.

4. Select **Run Continuously Until 'Esc'** check box.

Stop Continuous Run

Press **Esc** .... 〖Esc〗

Add Transitions

Add Transition in Slide Sorter View

1. Open presentation, or create new one.

2. Select slide to contain transition.

3. Click 〖⬚〗 or 〖No Transition〗

4. Select desired transition.

5. Click 〖   **OK**   〗 if necessary.

Set Slide Timing

Timings are set separately for each slide to advance slides automatically after the set amount of time. You may elect to set timing for some slides and leave others to advance manually. Slides for which timing is set can also be advanced manually.

Timing may be set manually or automatically using the new Rehearsal feature.

Set Timing Manually in Slide Sorter View

1. Open presentation, or create new one.

2. Click 〖⬚〗 on toolbar.

3. Select **Automatically After** option to choose automatic timing.

4. Type number .... *number* of seconds before advance.

5. Click 〖   **OK**   〗 .... 〖↵〗

Set Timing Automatically

1. Open presentation, or create new one.

2. Select **View, Slide Show** .... **Alt**+**V**,**W**

3. Select **Rehearse New Timings** button.

4. Click **Show** .... **Alt**+**S**

A dialog box appears in lower left corner during slide show to indicate amount of time you have displayed the slide.

—AFTER PRACTICING DIALOG FOR ACTIVE SLIDE—

5. Click **0:00:39** to advance to new slide and reset clock for next slide.

6. Repeat until all slides have been rehearsed.

7. Click **Yes** to accept practiced timings.

   OR

   Click **No** to discard timings.

Hide Slides

Hidden slides are part of a presentation, but are not shown unless needed. Hidden slides appear as an icon on the slide preceding them during the presentation.

Create Hidden Slide in Slide Sorter View

1. Display slide to hide.

2. Click 🖾 on toolbar.

A mark crosses out the slide number in Slide Sorter view.

Display Hidden Slide

Displays hidden slide during presentation slide show.

1. Open presentation, and start slide show.

   —WHEN SLIDE PRECEDING HIDDEN
   SLIDE APPEARS—

2. Type slide number .... *number*

3. Press **Enter** ....

   NOTE: When more than one consecutive slide is
   hidden, clicking the hidden slide icon
   activates all hidden slides following the
   active slide.

   To show specific hidden slides:

   Enter slide number to show and press **Enter** ....🔳

Annotate During Show

Allows you to write freehand on slides during presentations
without altering the slides. The freehand icon feature is a toggle
button used to turn the feature on and off.

1. Open presentation, and start slide show.

2. Click 🖊 (lower right corner) to turn annotation on.

   NOTE: Timings are suspended while annotation is
   being used.

3. Use mouse button to position pencil and write/draw.

4. Click 🖊 to turn annotation off.

Branch Slides

NOTE: This feature is available only in Windows
applications.

PowerPoint

Create New Presentation as Branch

NOTE: Branches may be created in Slide view and Notes Pages view only.

1. Open presentation, or create new one.
2. Display slide to contain branch.
3. Select **Insert**, **Object** .... Alt + I , O
4. Select **MS PowerPoint 4.0** in **Object Type** list box.
5. Select **Create New** option button.
6. Select **Display As Icon** check box option, if desired.
7. Click OK .... ↵
8. Prepare slides in new branch presentation.
9. Select **Window** .... Alt + W
10. Select original presentation.

NOTE: Branched icon should appear to indicate a branch is available. Move and size the icon, as desired.

Set Play Settings

1. Display slide on which you inserted branch.
2. Select branch icon to set play settings.
3. Select **Tools**, **Play Settings** .... Alt + T , Y
5. Select desired **Start Play** option.
6. Select **Hide While not Playing** check box option, if desired.
7. Click OK .... ↵

Run Branch

1. Open presentation containing branch, and start slide show.

2. Click presentation icon to branch to new presentation.

TEXT

> *NOTE:* The Slide view is used throughout this section, but the basic procedures presented here for formatting text, etc., apply to text entered in all accessible views. Procedures unique to specific views are included.

| Times New Roman | 24 | A A | B I U S | | |

Add Text in Slide View

Add Title

1. Click **Title** placeholder.

2. Type title text, pressing **Enter** .... ⏎
   to move to another line, or simply let text wrap.

> *NOTE:* To move to the body placeholder immediately after typing title, press *Ctrl+Enter* or click the body placeholder.

Add Body

1. Click body placeholder.

2. Type body text, pressing **Enter** .... ⏎
   to add another line and press **Tab** .... Tab
   to add subsections.

Add Text to Object

1. Select object to contain text.

2. Type text .... *text*

Using Text Tool

*The toolbar **text tool** is used to create a defined text box area or to add text to graphics and pictures. It can also be used to add text to the title and body objects. Adding text using the text tool allows typing without bullets and other formatting restrictions. Unless a text box is defined, text does not wrap to additional lines when the margin is reached.*

Text added using the text tool creates a text box object which can be moved as any other object on a PowerPoint slide.

Add Text in Slide View with Text Tool

1. Click ▣ on toolbar.

2. Position ╋ to begin typing.

3. Type text... *text*

> NOTE: *When using the text tool, PowerPoint does not wrap text onto the next line unless a text box is outlined before you start typing. It is necessary to press **Enter** to move to a new line.*

Create Defined Text Box

1. Click ▣ on toolbar.

2. Position ╋ in area to contain text box.

3. Click/drag until box outline occupies space for text.

4. Release mouse button.

When you release the mouse button, the text box appears the width of the box you defined, but only the depth (height) of one line of text is defined. The box, as you type, expands to fill the box outline.

5. Type text... *text*

Add Text to Graphic/Picture

The text tool must be used to add text to an imported graphic or picture.

Text may only be added using the text tool in the Slide view.

1. Click ⬚ on status bar.
2. Display slide containing graphic/picture.
3. Click [A] on tool palette.
4. Position ⊥ on graphic/picture to contain text.

   NOTE: If desired, you can outline the text box area before typing text.

5. Type text...*text*

Select Text

PowerPoint treats text as words, not characters. It is, therefore, sometimes possible to position the cursor within a word to format it, etc., without actually selecting the word.

Slide text can be selected in Slide view or Outline view only. Notes text can be selected in Notes Pages view only.

1. Click ⬚ or ☰ on status bar.
2. Position cursor on word/section to select.

   OR

   Position cursor on bulleted item until mouse pointer becomes a ✥

3. Click outline bulleted section or non–bulleted paragraph.

   OR

   Double–click to select word.

   OR

   Triple–click slide text to select non–bulleted paragraph.

   NOTE: A section includes all text for the bulleted item and subsidiary levels of that item.

Move Text

Reorganizes, rearranges or repositions text quickly and easily using the buttons available on PowerPoint's toolbars and tool palettes. Text can also be dragged to a new position or cut and pasted to a new location. PowerPoint 4.0 automatically adjusts leading and trailing spaces when text is moved.

Text can be moved only in Slide view or Outline view.

Move Text Up in Slide View

> *NOTE:*   *These steps are for text entered in Normal text mode rather than as graphic text using the text tool.*

1. Display slide to reorganize.

2. Select text to move.

3. Position pointer on selected text.

> *NOTE:*   *Mouse should be a ↖—not a ✛*

4. Click and drag text until vertical bar is properly positioned.

> *NOTE:*   *Mouse pointer carries a **small page icon** while text is being dragged. The line identifies new text location.*

5. Drop text.

6. Repeat steps 2–5 until all text is properly placed.

Move Text Down in Slide View

> *NOTE:*   *These steps are for text entered in Normal text mode rather than as graphic text using the text tool.*

1. Display slide to reorganize.

2. Select text to move.

3. Position pointer on selected text.

MOVE TEXT DOWN IN SLIDE VIEW (CONTINUED)

NOTE: *Mouse should be a ☖—not a ✥*

4. Click and drag text until vertical bar is properly positioned.

   NOTE: *Mouse pointer carries a **small page icon** while text is being dragged. The line identifies the new text location.*

5. Drop text.

6. Repeat steps 2–5 until all text is properly placed.

Move Text Left One Level (Promote)

1. Click ▣ or ▤ on status bar.

2. Display slide to reorganize.

3. Position I in line to move.

4. Click ◁ on toolbar.

5. Repeat step 4 until line is properly placed.

Move Text Right One Level (Demote)

1. Click ▣ or ▤ on status bar.

2. Display slide to reorganize.

3. Position I in line to move.

4. Click ▷ on toolbar.

5. Repeat step 4 until line is properly placed.

Drag Text (Promote/Demote)

1. Click ▣ or ▤ on status bar.

2. Display slide to reorganize.

3. Position pointer at left edge of first line of paragraph to move.

DRAG TEXT (PROMOTE/DEMOTE) (CONTINUED)

NOTE: The mouse pointer should become a ✛;
when you click, the entire item and all its
sublevels are selected. Text can be moved
in any direction. The direction of the first
movement determines up/down, left/right
move direction.

4. Drag text to new location and release mouse
button.

*As you drag, a line appears across the screen indicating the
current placement of the text.*

5. Repeat step 3 until line is properly placed.

NOTE: If you accidentally drop the text at the
wrong location, the Undo feature is the
quickest way to return it to its original
position.

Move Text Box

1. Click 🖥 on status bar.

2. Click ↖ on tool palette.

3. Select text box to move.

NOTE: It may be necessary to position the pointer
close to the outline around the text box
and click again to access handles.

4. Position pointer on text box edge and drag to move
to new location.

NOTE: Pointer should be an arrow—not an
I–beam. To obtain pointer mouse,
reposition the I–beam closer to the box
edge.

Copy Text

Copy/Paste

1. Select text to copy.
2. Click 🖺 .... `Ctrl`+`C`
3. Position cursor in new text location.
4. Click 🖺 .... `Ctrl`+`V`
5. Repeat step 4 for each position to contain text.

Edit Text

Slide text may not be edited in Notes view or Slide Sorter view.

Insert Text

> *NOTE:*   *PowerPoint is automatically in the Insert mode when adding text.*

1. Position ⌶ to insert new text.

> *NOTE:*   *If pointer is not an ⌶, double–click on text and then position I–beam.*

2. Type new text .... *text*

Delete Text

1. Position ⌶ before text to delete.

> *NOTE:*   *If pointer is not an I–beam, double–click text and then position I–beam.*

2. Press **Del** .... `Del`
3. Repeat steps 1–2 until all text is deleted.

Change Font

1. Click 🖾/🖽 on status bar.
2. Select text containing font to change.
3. Click font type box on toolbar ..... `Alt`+`O`,`F`,`F`
4. Select desired font.

Change Size

1. Click 🖵/🗐 on status bar.
2. Select text containing font size to change.
3. Click font type box on toolbar ..... Alt + O , F , F
4. Select desired size.

Enhance Text

Turn Enhancement On

1. Select text to enhance.
2. Click desired text enhancement toolbar button(s).

   OR

   a. Select **Format**, **Font**.................. Alt + O , F

   b. Select desired enhancement.

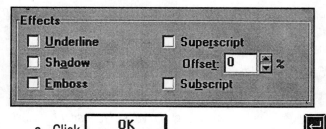

   c. Click [OK] .... ↵

3. Click neutral position to deselect text.

Emboss Text Object

Creates an embossed appearance to the object box, or gives text a raised appearance. A shadowed text object creates a sharper embossed image.

Emboss Text

1. Display Drawing+ toolbar.
2. Select text to emboss.
3. Click 🖼️ .... Alt + O , F
4. Select Emboss(ed) .... Alt + E
5. Click [OK] if necessary.

Spell Check Text

Checks spelling of all words in presentation slides and handouts. Words, such as proper names, that you use frequently can be added to the dictionary. Text in graphics, charts and other objects is not checked. See Spell Check in Word section.

Find and Replace

Searches slides, outlines, notes and handouts in a presentation for text to be replaced. Text on pictures and imported objects is not searched.

*See Find and Replace in **Word** section.*

TABS

*PowerPoint sets up horizontal and vertical rulers for both text and graphics. The **text ruler** displays the settings for indents and tabs and is available only in Slide and Notes view. The text ruler measures from the left while the **graphic ruler** measures in both directions from the slide center.*

PowerPoint # POWERPOINT # POWERPOINT 235

TABS (CONTINUED)

*PowerPoint's default tabs fall every inch after the last indent. They appear as faint shadows on the line below the scale. As with other applications, there are four different types of tabs which may be selected by clicking the **Tab** button to the left of the horizontal ruler until the desired tab type is shown:*

TAB TYPE:	BUTTON:	DESCRIPTION:
Left		Aligns text at the left and types right.
Right	L	Aligns text at the right and types left.
Center	⅃	Center text around the tab stop.
Decimal	⊥	Centers text around the decimal
	⊥	point.

Show/Hide Ruler

Click 🖳 or 🖳 on status bar.............. `Alt`+`V`,`R`

> *NOTE: A check mark to the left of ruler indicates it is active when in the Slide or Notes view.*

Set Tab

1. Show ruler for text or text object.
2. Position cursor in text or text object.
3. Click desired tab button to left of horizontal ruler until desired tab type appears
4. Click ruler at position for tab.

> *NOTE: PowerPoint removes all default tabs before the one you set.*

Move Tabs

1. Position pointer on tab to move.
2. Click and drag tab to new position.
3. Release mouse button.

Change Default Tabs

1. Click ⬚ on status bar.

2. Display ruler.

3. Position cursor in text or text object for which to change default tabs.

4. Click desired default tab marker and drag to new location.

   NOTE: *Space between all default tab markers changes proportionately. To set varied tabs, they must be placed individually.*

Remove Tabs

NOTE: *Default tabs cannot be removed by this procedure. Default tabs positioned before a manually set tab are removed when the new tab is set and restored when the manually set tab is removed.*

1. Click ⬚ on status bar.

2. Display ruler.

3. Position cursor in text or text object from which to remove tab.

4. Position pointer on tab to remove and drag from ruler.

5. Release mouse button.

INDENTS

*An indent is a temporary margin for a paragraph. It remains in effect until **Tab**, **Shift+Tab** or **Enter** is pressed. PowerPoint allows up to five indents to be set for each text block or object. Bullet lists use indents to align text for point levels. The ruler displays a pair of markers for each bulleted item level available.*

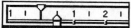

The top marker on the scale represents the placement for the first line of a paragraph. The marker on the bottom of the scale represents the placement for carryover lines of a paragraph. For bulleted items, the top marker indicates the placement of the bullet. The square below the bottom marker can be moved without altering the placement of the first line in relation to the carryover lines.

Set Indent

PowerPoint comes with default settings for five different levels of indents (the maximum).

Adjust Indent

1. Select object containing indent to adjust.
2. Click ⬚ on status bar.
3. Display ruler.
4. Drag upper or lower marker until text is properly placed.

   NOTE: If the upper marker moves with the bottom marker, it maintains the indent relatively. To move the bottom marker separately, it is necessary to place the pointer precisely on the marker rather than on the square below the bottom marker. The top marker can be moved independently to adjust the indent distances.

Move Text Maintaining Relative Indent

1. Select object containing indent to move.

2. Click 🖳 on status bar.

3. Display ruler.

4. Drag square below bottom marker to reposition both upper and lower markers to new position.

Remove Indent

Drag top or bottom marker until it is aligned with its counterpart (component marker).

LINE SPACING

1. Click 🖳 on status bar.

2. Position cursor within paragraph text to change.

3. Select **Format, Line Spacing**.......... `Alt`+`O`,`S`

5. Double–click to select spacing to change.

6. Select **Lines** or **Points** from text box to right of spacing settings.

7. Click `Preview` to view changes........ `Alt`+`P`

8. Click `OK` .... `↵`

Align Text

1. Select text to align.

2. Select **Format, Alignment** .... `Alt`+`O`,`A`

3. Select desired alignment option.

Align Text Objects

1. Using **Shift+***click*, select text and other object(s) to align.

   *NOTE: If text has been added to a drawn,
   imported or graphic object, it may be
   necessary to group the objects before
   continuing.*

2. Select **D**raw, **A**lign .... Alt + D , A
3. Select desired alignment option.

Fit Text

*Allows you to arrange text within a text box or object the way
you want it to appear. It can be arranged at the top of the box,
in the center or toward the bottom of a box by changing the
anchor point. The text box can be sized to accommodate the
text, and **word wrap** can be turned on/off from the Fit Text
dialog box, where you can also set the margins.*

Anchor Text

1. Select object containing text.
2. Select **F**ormat, **T**ext Anchor .... Alt + O , T
3. Select **Anchor P**oint text box.
4. Select desired position.
5. Click **Preview** .... Alt + P
   to view change.
6. Click **OK** .... ↵

Size Text Object Automatically

1. Select object containing text.

2. Select **Format, Text Anchor**............ `Alt`+`O`,`T`

3. Select **Adjust Object Size to Fit Text** check box option, if desired.

4. Click `Preview` to view change.......... `Alt`+`P`

5. Click `OK` .... `↵`

Word Wrap On/Off

1. Select object containing text.

2. Click **Format, Text Anchor**.............. `Alt`+`O`,`T`

3. Select **Word–wrap Text in Object** check box option, if desired.

4. Click `Preview` to view change.......... `Alt`+`P`

5. Click `OK` .... `↵`

MARGINS

1. Select object containing text.

2. Select **Format, Text Anchor**............ `Alt`+`O`,`T`

3. Double–click top **Box Margins** text box to change left/right margins.

4. Double–click bottom **Box Margins** text box to change top/bottom margins.

NOTE: Margins must be set individually for each text box/object.

MARGINS (CONTINUED)

5. Click [Preview] .... `Alt`+`P`
   to view change.

6. Click [OK] .... ⏎

TOOLBARS

PowerPoint provides seven toolbars grouping features commonly used to perform specific tasks. Each toolbar can be edited to meet your needs, and additional toolbars can be created to customize special features.

Display/Hide Toolbar

1. Select **V**iew, **T**oolbars .... `Alt`+`V`, `T`

Toolbars:	
☑ **Standard**	OK
☑ Formatting	Cancel
☐ Custom	
☑ Drawing	Reset
☑ Drawing+	Customize...
☐ Microsoft	
☐ AutoShapes	Help

☒ Color Buttons   ☒ Show ToolTips

2. Select desired **T**oolbars to display/remove.

3. Click [OK] .... ⏎

UNDO

Click ↶ .... `Alt`+`E`, `U`

> *NOTE: Only the last action is reversed.*

VIEWS

PowerPoint allows four different views for working with presentations, notes, handouts, outlines and slides.

Change View

Click desired status bar view button:

- 🔲   Slide view
- 📄   Outline view
- 💻   Notes view
- 🔡   Slide Sorter view

WIZARDS

AutoContent Wizard

1. Select **AutoContent Wizard**.................... **Alt**+**A**
   in PowerPoint window.

2. Click [**OK**] .... **↵**

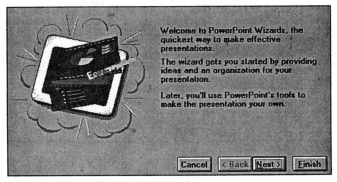

3. Select desired option button.

5. Type information for each screen presented.

6. Click [**Finish**] to create presentation .... **Alt**+**F**

Pick a Look Wizard

1. Select **Pick a Look Wizard** .... `Alt`+`P`
   in **PowerPoint** window.

2. Click [OK   ] .... `↵`

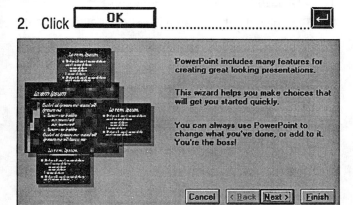

3. Select desired option button.

4. Select options, as prompted, for each screen
   presented.

5. Click [**Finish**] to create presentation..... `Alt`+`F`

DATABASE

Create New Database

1. Click [New] .... Alt+F, N
2. Type new database name................ *database name*
3. Click OK .... ↵

Open Database

1. Click [Open] .... Alt+F, O
2. Type desired **File Name** .... *filename*
3. Click OK .... ↵

The Database Window

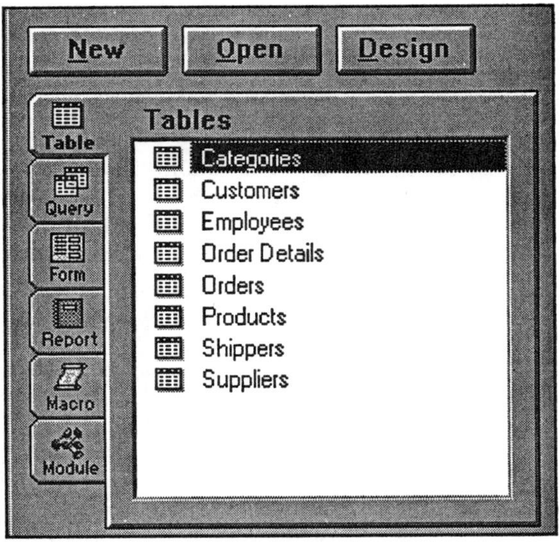

Create Object

Creates tables, queries, forms, reports, macros and modules.

1. View Database window.
2. Click desired object type button to create.
3. Click | **New** | .... `Alt`+`N`
4. Click **New (object name)** .... `N`
   to create object manually.
   OR

   Click **(object name) Wizard** .... `W`
   to create object with help.

Open Object

1. View Database window.
2. Click desired object type button to open.
3. Click **Open** .... `Alt`+`O`

Copy Object

1. View Database window.
2. Click desired object type button to copy.
3. Select object... `↓`
4. Select **Edit**, **Copy** .... `Alt`+`E`,`C`
5. View Database window of destination database.
6. Select **Edit**, **Paste**........................ `Alt`+`E`,`P`
7. Type name for pasted object .... *object name*
8. Select desired option for pasted table.
9. Click | **OK** | .... `↵`

Rename Object

1. View Database window
2. Click desired object type button to rename.
3. Select object .... ⬇
4. Select **File, Rename** .... Alt + F , M
5. Type new name.. *name*
6. Click ⌷ OK ⌷ .... ⏎

Delete Object

1. Select object to delete in Database window.
2. Select **Edit, Delete** .... Alt + E , E
3. Click ⌷ OK ⌷ .... ⏎

Print Definition of Database Object

1. Select desired object in Database window.
2. Select **File Print Definition** .... Alt + F , F
3. Specify desired options for chosen definition.
4. Click ⌷ OK ⌷ .... ⏎

Open Zoom Box

1. Place insertion point in desired text box.
2. Press **Shift+F2** .... Shift + F2
3. View or edit contents of text box.
4. Click ⌷ OK ⌷ .... ⏎

Display Property Sheet

Displays property sheet in design views of forms, reports or queries where control and section properties may be customized. The property sheet will change depending on the control or section selected.

1. Click or select control, section or window desired in Design view of form report or query.
2. Click 🖼 .... `Alt`+`V`, `P`

TABLES

Create Table

1. Click [⊞ Table] in Database window... `Alt`+`V`, `T`
2. Click [**New**] .... `Alt`+`N`
3. Click [□] .... `N`

Add Fields

1. Click in top available **Field Name** area, if necessary.
2. Type new field name .... *field name*

   NOTE: *Field names may be up to 64 characters long.*

3. Press **Tab** .... `Tab`
4. Click drop–down arrow .... `Alt`+`↓`
5. Select data type .... `↓`
6. Press **Tab** .... `Tab`
7. Type description, if desired.
8. Press **Tab** .... `Tab`

Data Types

Text	Contains alphanumeric characters; up to 255 characters.
Memo	Contains alphanumeric characters; up to 64,000 bytes.
Number	Contains integers or fractional values; 1, 2, 4 or 8 bytes.
Date/Time	Contains date and time values; 8 bytes.
Currency	Contains monetary values; 8 bytes.
Counter	Contains an automatically incremented numeric value; 4 bytes.
Yes/No	Contains Boolean values; 1 bit.
OLE Object	Contains OLE (Object Linking and Embedding) objects, graphics, binary data; up to 1 gigabit/gigabyte.

Move Field

1. Click the field selector (to left of field name).
2. Click and drag field selector to new location.

Delete Field

1. Click field selector.
2. Press **Delete** .... Del

Set Primary Key

1. Click desired field to use.
2. Click ☞ .... Alt + E , S

ACCESS   249

Set Multiple Field Primary Key

1. Click field indicator (to left of field name) for first field to use.

2. Press **Ctrl** .... `Ctrl`
   and click field indicator for additional field to use.

3. Click ▤ .... `Alt`+`E`

4. Choose **Set Primary Key** .... `S`

Save Table

1. Select **File**, **Save** .... `Alt`+`F`, `S`

2. Type table name if necessary ....*table name*

3. Click ▭ **OK** .... `↵`

Add Records to New Table

1. View desired table.

2. Click **Datasheet View** ▦

3. Type data in first field .... *data*

4. Press **Tab** .... `Tab`

5. Type data in next field .... *data*

6. Repeat steps 4–5, as necessary.

Open Table

Open a Table in Datasheet View

1. Click ▦ `Table` in Database window.

2. Double–click table name to open.

Open a Table in Design View

1. Click ⊞ Table in Database window.
2. Select table.
3. Click **Design** .... Alt + D

Set Field Properties
Limit Text Field Size

1. Open table in Design view.
2. Select desired field.............................. ↑ ↓
3. Press **F6** F6
4. Type maximum number of characters (1–255).

Limit Field Size for Number Data Type

1. Open table in Design view.
2. Select desired field.............................. ↑ ↓
3. Press **F6** F6
4. Type desired number data type.

Display Formats
Set Number Format

1. Open table in Design view.
2. Select number field to format.
3. Click **Format** text box................... F6, ↓
4. Select desired number format .... Alt + ↓, ↓

Set Date or Time Format

1. Open table in Design view.
2. Select date/time field to format.
3. Click **Format** text box .... `F6`,`↓`
4. Select desired date/time format...... `Alt`+`↓`,`↓`

Set Yes/No Format

1. Open table in Design view.
2. Select yes/no field to format.
3. Click **Format** text box .... `F6`,`↓`
4. Select desired yes/no format.......... `Alt`+`↓`,`↓`

Set Default Values for Fields

Existing forms are not affected when default values are specified in a table.

1. View database table in Design view.
2. Select desired field.
3. Click **Default Value** text box.................. `F6`,`↓`
4. Type desired default value.

    NOTE: *Expressions may be entered if preceded by an equal sign. See **Expressions**, page 322, and **Expression Builder**, page 323.*

Set Validation Rules

1. View database table in Design view.
2. Select desired field.
3. Click **Validation Rule** text box .... `F6`,`↓`
4. Type validation expression.
5. Click **Validation Text** text box .... `↓`
6. Type error message used for invalid entry.

Create Index

Create Index on Single Field

1. Open table in Design view.
2. Select field to index.
3. Click **Indexed** text box .... `F6`, `↓`
4. Click drop–down arrow .... `Alt`+`↓`
   to select desired index type.

Create Multiple Field Index

1. Open table in Design view.
2. Click 📝 .... `Alt`+`V`, `I`
3. Type **Index Name** .... `↓`, *index name*
4. Type/select **Field Name** .... `Tab`, `Alt`+`↓`
5. Select **Sort Order** .... `Tab`, `Alt`+`↓`
6. Click **Field Name** text box in row just below .. `Tab`
7. Repeat steps 4–6.

   *NOTE: Leave **Index Name** text box for the row blank.*

11. Double–click ⬛ to close .... `Alt`+`Space`, `C`

Create Input Mask

Automatically displays formatting characters in a field. Data is entered by filling the blanks in the input mask. An input mask used in a field in a table will also be used in forms and reports that use controls bound to that field. Input masks may be created for controls in forms and reports.

(CONTINUED)

1. Open table in Design view.
2. Select desired field.
3. Click **Input Mask** text box .... F6 , ↓
4. Type desired input mask using keyboard text and special characters.

Set Relationship Between Tables

Allows Access to use data from more than one table at a time. Relationships may be one–to–one or one–to–many (a many–to–many relationship incorporates a one–to–many linking table). Once table relationships are set, referential integrity may be enforced. This ensures that data related to data in another table may not be deleted.

1. View Database window.
2. Click 🔗 .... Alt + E , R
3. Select desired **Table/Query** .... ↓
4. Click **Add** .... A
5. Repeat steps 4–5 for additional table(s) to add.
6. Click **Close** when finished C
7. Place pointer on desired field in primary table.
8. Click and drag field to desired related field in secondary table.
9. Release mouse button.
10. Click **Enforce Referential Integrity** .... Alt + E if desired.

(CONTINUED)

NOTE: *Ensures that relationships between records
are valid, and that related data cannot be
accidentally deleted. Can be used only
when (a) the matching field from the
primary table is a primary key or has a
unique index, (b) the related fields have the
same data type and (c) both tables belong
to the same Access database.*

11. Select desired relationship type.

12. Select **Create** .... 🄲

View Relationships

1. View Database window.

2. Click 🖳 .... **Alt**+**E**,**R**

3. Select **Relationships** menu .... **Alt**+**R**
   if desired.

4. Select **Show All** .... **L**
   to view all relationships.

   OR

   Select **Show Direct** .... **D**
   to view relationships for selected table only.

Edit Relationship

1. View Database window.

2. Click 🖳 .... **Alt**+**E**,**R**

3. Double–click relationship line to edit.

Delete Relationship
1. View Database window.
2. Click 🖼 .... Alt + E, R
3. Click relationship line to delete.
4. Press **Delete** .... Del

Delete Table from Relationship Window
1. View Database window.
2. Click 🖼 .... Alt + E, R
3. Select table to remove.
4. Press **Delete** .... Del

Export Data from Access
1. Select **File**, **Export** .... Alt + F, E
2. Select database export format from **Data Destination** list box.
3. Click [OK] .... ↵
4. Select table to export .... ↓
5. Click [OK] .... ↵
6. Type filename for exported file .... *filename*
7. Click [OK] twice .... ↵, ↵

QUERIES

Display selected data from a database – may be used to limit fields, select specific records, sort records, find information from several tables, and perform calculations. Forms, reports, graphs, and other queries may be based on queries. The result of a select query is a dynaset, which is a temporary set, not stored, made up of data from the database. Action queries can delete, append, project and update data in tables.

Create Query

1. Click [Query] in Database window.... `Alt`+`V`, `Q`

2. Click **N**ew.. `Alt`+`N`

3. Click **N**ew **Query** .... `N`

4. Select desired category to display.

5. Select **Table/Query** to include .... `Alt`+`T`, `↓`

6. Click **A**dd.. `↵`

7. Repeat steps 4–5 for each table or query to add.

8. Click **Close** .... `Esc`

Save Query

1. Click 🖫............................... `Alt`+`F`, `S`

2. Type query name ....*name*
   if saving query for the first time.

   *NOTE: Don't give a query the same name as an
   existing table unless you want to replace it.*

3. Click **OK** .... `↵`

Open Query
Design View

1. Click 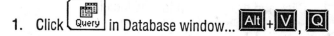 in Database window... `Alt`+`V`, `Q`

2. Select query to open in Query window ....`↓`

3. Click **D**esign ....`Alt`+`D`

Datasheet View

NOTE: Query must have at least one output field.

1. Click ⬚Query in Database window... `Alt`+`V`, `Q`

2. Double–click query to open in Query window.

Add Fields
Add Single Field

1. Click and drag the field name from the field list to a cell in the Field row of the QBE grid.

2. Repeat for additional fields.

Add Several Fields

1. Press **Ctrl** ....`Ctrl`
   and click each field to include in field list.

2. Drag group to QBE grid.

Add All Fields

1. Double–click title bar of field list.

2. Drag group to QBE grid.

Move Field

1. Click desired field selector bar above field name.

2. Click and drag column to new location.

Insert Field

1. Click desired field in field list box.

2. Drag field to desired cell in QBE grid.

Existing fields shift to right.

Delete Field

1. Click field selector bar above field name.

2. Press **Delete**... `Del`

Delete All Fields

Select **Edit, Clear Grid** .... `Alt`+`E`, `A`

Change Column Widths

1. Place pointer on right edge of field selector of column to resize.

2. Click and drag border to desired size.

    OR
    Double–click to adjust column automatically.

Display Table Names in QBE Grid

Select **View, Table Names**.................. `Alt`+`V`, `N`

View Query's Datasheet

Displays the result of a select or crosstab query. The set of records shown is the dynaset.

Click 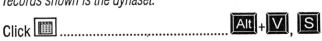 .... `Alt`+`V`, `S`

View Datasheet's Query

> *NOTE:* *Each time a query is edited, a new dynaset (set of records) is created.*

Click 📝... **Alt** + **V**, **D**

Cancel Query

Press **Ctrl+Break** .... **Ctrl** + **Break**

Change Data in Query's Datasheet

> *NOTE:* *Data may be edited in a query datasheet, although calculated fields will not be in effect. If desired, a form may be created to change data in a datasheet (see **Forms**, page 264).*

Rename Field in Datasheet

> *NOTE:* *Use this technique to change the name displayed on the datasheet view, form or report based on the query: the table field name remains the same.*

1. Click to left of first letter of field name in QBE grid in Design view.

2. Type new field name .... *fieldname* **:** followed by a colon (:).

New name is added before field name.

Update Datasheet when Data Has Been Changed

Press **Shift+F9**.. **Shift** + **F9**

Specify Criteria for Field

1. Click **Criteria** cell for desired field .... ⬇️
   in QBE grid.

2. Type data to match or an expression.

3. Press **Shift+F2** .... Shift + F2
   to view long expression.

Enter Values as Criteria

Numbers	Enter digits with decimals only. Do not use currency symbols, commas or other characters.
Dates	Dates may be entered in any standard format. If using a date as part of an expression, enclose it in number signs, for example: #4/15/94#.
Text	If entering text that contains commas or spaces, enclose the whole entry in quotation marks, for example: "for sale".
Yes/No	Use Yes, True, On, −1 or No, False, Off or 0.

Specify Sort Order

> *NOTE: If a sort on several fields is specified, the fields are sorted in priority from left to right (see **Move Field**, page 248).*

1. Click Sort cell for desired field .... ⬇️
   in QBE grid.

2. Click drop-down arrow .... Alt + ⬇️

3. Choose desired sort order.

4. Repeat steps 1–3 for each desired field to sort.

Exclude Field from Dynaset

Click Show check box to clear in QBE grid.

Sort or Add Criteria to Query Using Asterisk

1. Add fields to use for sort or criteria to query based on asterisk (*).

2. Add criteria.

3. Click each added table's **Show** check box to clear.

Add Table to Query

1. Click ⊞ .... `Alt`+`Q`, `A`

2. Select table to add .... `↓`

3. Select **Add** .... `↵`

4. Repeat steps 2–3 for each table to add.

5. Click **Close** .... `C`

Delete Table from Query

1. Select table.

2. Press **Delete** .... `Del`

Create Calculated Fields

Display values calculated from number or date fields, or values concatenated from text fields.

1. View query in Design view.

2. Place insertion point in empty Field cell.

3. Type expression enclosing field names in square brackets.
   EXAMPLES: [city]&", "&[state], or
   [quantity 1]+[quantity 2].

CREATE CALCULATED FIELDS (CONTINUED)

4. Press **Tab** to enter expression ....[Tab]

5. Open **Zoom** box to view long expression..[Shift]+[F2].

6. Click and drag pointer to select default name to use a name other than the default expression name.

7. Type new name.................................*name*

Create Crosstab Query

Use field values as column or row headings.

1. Create query (*see Create Query, page 256*).

2. Select **Query, Crosstab**...................[Alt]+[Q],[B]

3. Click Crosstab cell in desired field to use as row heading.

4. Select **Row Heading** ....[Alt]+[↓], [↓]

5. Repeat steps 3-4, to add additional row headings, if desired.

   NOTE: The total for at least one row heading field must be set to Group By.

6. Click **Crosstab** cell in desired field to use as column heading.

7. Select **Column Heading**...............[Alt]+[↓], [↓]

   NOTE: Only one column heading may be chosen. The Total for the field must be set to Group By.

8. Click **Crosstab** cell in desired field to use as summary values.

9. Select **Value** ....[Alt]+[↓], [↓]

10. Click **Total** cell in same field.

11. Select desired type of total ....[Alt]+[↓]

    NOTE: Group By can not be used.

12. Click [▦] to view dynaset ....[Alt]+[V], [S]

Use Query to Create Form or Report

*NOTE: Queries control data that can be viewed in
a form or report. Queries may also be used
as the basis for a form to enter or edit
data, but some values may not be able to
be edited.*

QUERY/FIELD TYPE:	CHANGEABLE?
Query—one table	Yes
Query—two tables, one–to–one	Yes
Query—two tables, one–to–many	Usually
Query with totals	No
Query—one–to–one self join	No
Query with unique values set to yes	No
Query–crosstab	No
Field–calculated	No
Query–union	No
Query – pass through	No
Read–only field	No
Query with attached table with no unique index or primary key	No

Create Parameter Query

*Allows the user to enter changing criteria in frequently used
queries without opening the QBE grid. May be used as the
basis of forms or reports.*

1. Create a query *(see **Create Query,** page 256).*
   NOTE: Do not use the Wizard to create the query.
2. Click **Criteria** cell of QBE grid of field to use as
   parameter.
3. Type desired text to use as prompt ... *[prompt text]*
   enclosed in square brackets.
   *NOTE: Prompt text cannot match field name, but
   may contain field name,
   for example: [Enter the zip code:].*
4. Click 🖩 to test.

CREATE PARAMETER QUERY (CONTINUED)

5. Type value or text .... *value*
   as indicated by step 3.

6. Click [**OK**   ] .... [↵]

FORMS

Create Form with FormWizard

> *NOTE:*   *Use FormWizard to create a form which*
> *can be customized automatically.*

1. Click [⊞ Form] in Database window... [Alt]+[V], [F]

2. Click [**New**] .... [Alt]+[N]

3. Click drop–down arrow........................... [Alt]+[↓]
   to select a table or query.

4. Click [⊞🖐] .... [Alt]+[W]

5. Select desired form style .... [↓]

6. Click [**OK**   ] .... [↵]

7. Follow screen instructions for specific form type.

Create Blank Form

1. Click [⊞ Form] in Database window... [Alt]+[V], [F]

2. Click [**New**] .... [Alt]+[N]

3. Click drop–down arrow .... [Alt]+[↓]
   to select table or query.

4. Click [☐] .... [Alt]+[B]

Select Controls

NOTE: A control is a graphical object that may be placed on a form to display data, label data, decorate or perform an action.

Select Single Control

Click the control.

NOTE: If the control has an attached label, or the label has an attached text box, combo box or check box, a move handle appears on the attached object as well as the clicked control.

Select Adjacent Controls

1. Position insertion point at outside corner of group to select.

2. Click and drag rectangle to enclose or intersect with controls to include.

Select Nonadjacent or Overlapping Controls

1. Click first control to select.

2. Hold down **Shift** key .... `Shift`
   and click additional controls to select.

Move Controls

Move Control with Label

1. Select control to move.

2. Place pointer at a border of the control.

3. Drag the control to the new location.

NOTE: Attached label will move with control.

Move Control Only

1. Select control to move.

2. Place pointer on move handle at upper left corner.

3. Drag control to new location.

Restrict Movement of Control

Keeps controls aligned vertically or horizontally.

1. Press and hold **Shift** ....`Shift`

2. Click to select each control to move, holding mouse button down when selecting the last one.

3. Drag controls to new horizontal or vertical location.

Move Enclosed Controls

Moves controls enclosed by other controls, such as a rectangle enclosing a group of related controls.

1. Select **V**iew, **O**ptions ....`Alt`+`V`, `O`

2. Select **Form & Report Design** ....`↓` in **C**ategory list box.

3. Select **Move Enclosed Controls**.....`Alt`+`↓`, `↓` in **I**tems list box.

4. Set to `Yes` ....`Y`

5. Click `OK` ....`↵`

6. Select the enclosing control.

7. Place insertion point on control anywhere but on the move handle.

8. Click and drag group to a new location.

Attach Label

1. Click $\boxed{\textbf{A}}$ in tool box.
2. Click pointer where label is to appear.
3. Type label text ....*label text*
4. Select label .... $\boxed{\hookleftarrow}$
5. Select **Edit**, **Cut** .... $\boxed{\text{Alt}}$+$\boxed{\text{E}}$,$\boxed{\text{T}}$
6. Select desired control.
7. Select **Edit**, **Paste** .... $\boxed{\text{Alt}}$+$\boxed{\text{E}}$,$\boxed{\text{P}}$
8. Adjust placement.

Align Controls

1. Select controls to align.
2. Select **Format**, **Align** .... $\boxed{\text{Alt}}$+$\boxed{\text{O}}$,$\boxed{\text{A}}$
3. Choose desired edge alignment option.

Turn Snap to Grid On/Off

Aligns newly created controls with an invisible grid.

Select **Format**, **Snap to Grid** .... $\boxed{\text{Alt}}$+$\boxed{\text{O}}$,$\boxed{\text{G}}$
to select or clear.

Change Space Between Controls

1. Select controls to space.
2. Select **Format** menu .... $\boxed{\text{Alt}}$+$\boxed{\text{O}}$
3. Choose desired spacing option.
4. Choose desired controls spacing option.

268 ACCESS

Save Form

1. Select **F**ile, **S**ave .... `Alt`+`F`,`S`

2. Type form name .... *form name*
   if saving for first time.

3. Click `OK` .... `↵`

Close Form

1. Select **F**ile menu................................ `Alt`+`F`

2. Click `Close` .... `C`

Add Field to Form

> *NOTE:* A control added to a form from a field list
> is known as a **bound control**. It is used to
> display, enter and edit values.

1. Open form in Design view.

2. Click 🗒 .... `Alt`+`V`, `L`

3. Select desired field(s) from list.

> *NOTES:* To select a consecutive group of fields,
> click the first field, hold **Shift** and click the
> last one.
>
> To select several fields, click the first field,
> hold **Ctrl** and click additional fields.

4. Drag fields to form, positioning top left corner of
   pointer, which will appear as a rectangle, where top
   left corner of first control is desired.

Add Unbound Control to Form

NOTE: *An unbound control is not connected to a field or expression and is used to display information or graphic elements. It may also be used to accept input that will not be stored in tables.*

1. Open form in Design view.
2. Click **abl** in tool box.
3. Click form at desired location of default size text box.

   OR

   Click and drag pointer at desired location on form.

Create Label

1. Open form in Design view.
2. Click **A** in tool box.
3. Click form at desired location of default size text box.

   OR

   Click and drag pointer at desired location on form.
4. Type desired text .... *text*
5. Press **Enter** ....

Edit Label

1. Select label to edit.
2. Place pointer at desired location in text, or select text to replace.
3. Type new text .... *text*
4. Press **Enter** ....

Create Calculated Text Box

> *NOTE: An expression in a text box on a form is not stored in the database, but calculated each time the form is displayed. (See **Expressions**, see page 322.)*

1. Open form in Design view.

2. Click ⌷abl⌷ in tool box.

3. Click form at desired location of default size text box.

   OR
   Click and drag pointer at desired location on form.

4. Click inside text box.

5. Type **equal sign** (=) .... 🔲

6. Type desired expression.

7. Press **Enter** .... 🔲

Control Properties
Display Property Sheet

> *NOTE: The contents of the property sheet vary depending on control type selected.*

Place pointer on control and double–click.

OR
1. Select control.

2. Click .... Alt + V , P

Change Control Properties

1. Select control.

2. Display property sheet *(see above)*.

3. Click drop–down arrow to select desired property category.

   (See **Macros**, *page 318.)*
   NOTE: Properties vary depending on type of control selected.

4. Click desired property text box...................... ⬇️

5. Type desired value... *value*
   OR

   Click drop–down arrow .... `Alt`+⬇️
   and make selection.

6. Repeat steps 4–5 for each property change.

7. Click 🖼 to close. .... `Alt`+`V`, `I`

Set Default Properties for Controls

1. Display any control property sheet.

2. Click desired control tool in the tool box.

3. Click drop–down arrow to select desired property category in Default property sheet.

   NOTE: Properties vary depending on selected control type.

4. Click desired property text box...................... ⬇️

5. Type desired value................................ `Alt`+⬇️

6. Repeat steps 4–5 for each property change.

7. Click 🖼 to close .... `Alt`+`V`, `I`

Change Properties of Several Controls

1. Display first control's property sheet.

2. Hold **Shift** .... Shift
   and select other controls to change.

3. In Multiple Selection property sheet, click drop–
   down arrow to select desired property category.

   *NOTE: Properties vary depending on selected
            control type.*

4. Click desired property text box .... ↓

5. Type desired value .... Alt + ↓

6. Repeat steps 4–5 for each property change.

7. Click 🖾 to close.......................... Alt + V , I

Control Property Sheet Information

   *NOTE: Because of field type and other variables,
            not all property sheets will contain all
            options listed below. Information about
            currently selected property appears on the
            status line at the bottom of the Access
            window.*

List Boxes and Combo Boxes

*Provides a list of values from which the user may select to
enter data in a field. A list box may be more than one column
and choices are always displayed. A combo box list is not
displayed until it is activated. Combo boxes may also contain a
user typed value.*

Create List or Combo Box Using the Control Wizard

1. Click 🖾 in tool box .... **Alt** + **V**, **W**

2. Click desired tool box tool.

3. Click form at desired location.

4. Follow instructions in dialog boxes.

Create List or Combo Box Manually

1. Click 🖾 .... **Alt** + **V**, **W**
   in tool box to deselect, if necessary.

2. Click **List Box** 🖾 or **Combo Box** 🖾 tool.

3. Click form at desired location to create unbound
   control.

   OR

   a. Click **Field List** 🖾 to create control bound to
      field.

   b. Drag field to form at desired location.

Create Check Box, Option (Radio) Button or Toggle Button

> *NOTE: Option buttons and toggle buttons are
> usually used in option groups (see below).
> Check boxes often stand alone.*

1. Click desired tool box tool.

2. Click 🖾 to display.

3. Click desired field.

4. Click desired location of upper left corner of field on form.

5. Double–click 🖾 of field list to close.

Add Picture or Caption to Face of Toggle or Command Button

1. Double–click button to open toggle or command button property sheet in Design view.

2. Choose **Layout Properties** category.

3. Type desired text in **Caption** text box.

   OR

   Type bitmap file path and name in **Picture** text box.

4. Double–click ⬛ to close............. `Alt`+`Shift`,`C`

Create Bound Option Group

Creates a group of check boxes, option buttons or toggle buttons, only one of which can be selected at one time.

Create Bound Option Group Using Wizard

1. Select **View** menu.................................. `Alt`+`V`

2. Click 🖾 in tool box....................................... `W`

3. Click 🔘 in tool box.

4. Click form at desired upper left corner of group.

5. Follow instructions in Option Group Wizard dialog boxes.

Create Bound Option Group Manually

1. Select **View** menu.................................. `Alt`+`V`

2. Select **Control Wizards** to clear, if necessary .. `W`

3. Click 🔳 to display.

4. Click 🔘 in tool box.

CREATE BOUND OPTION GROUP USING WIZARD (CONTINUED)

5. Drag field from field list to form.
6. Click desired field type tool box tool.
7. Place pointer inside option group at upper left corner of desired field location (group box should highlight).
8. Click to place field.
9. Repeat steps 6–8 for each field to add.
10. Double–click ⬜ .... **Alt**+**Shift**, **C** of field list to close.

     NOTE: Each control in a group receives a sequential option value beginning with 1 and noted on the control's property sheet. The option value is added to the underlying table when a button is selected in Form view. If controls are created outside the option group and then cut and pasted inside, the option value must be set manually.

Create Command Button

Initiates an action or set of actions and connects to macros or Access Basic functions.

Create Command Using Wizard

1. Select **View** menu .... **Alt**+**V**
2. Click ⬜ in tool box .... **W**
3. Click ⬜ in tool box.
4. Click form at desired upper left corner of command button.
5. Follow directions in **Command Button Wizard** dialog boxes.

Create Command Button Manually

1. Select **View** menu .... `Alt`+`V`

2. Select **Control Wizards** if necessary ...... `Alt`+`W`

3. Click **Command button** ⬜ .... `W`
   in tool box to clear, if necessary.

4. Click form at desired upper left corner location.

5. Click **Properties** 🖼 in tool box to display property sheet.

   —IN ON CLICK TEXT BOX—

6. Type name of macro .... *macro name*
   OR
   Click **Build** ⬛ to create new macro or event.
   *(See **Macros**, page 318.)*

7. Double–click ⬛ .... `Alt`+`Shift`, `C`
   of property sheet to close.

Create Unbound Control for User Input

Used on forms as labels, lines and boxes and cannot be used to input values in a table. Some unbound controls can be designed to start actions from the Form view, such as selecting reports to print.

1. Select **View** menu .... `Alt`+`V`

2. Select **Control Wizards** to clear, if necessary.

3. Click desired control type tool in tool box

4. Click form at desired upper left corner location.

5. Double–click control to open property sheet.

6. Choose **All Properties** category.

CREATE UNBOUND CONTROL FOR USER INPUT (CONTINUED)

7. Type name of control .... *control name*
   in **Name** text box.

8. Select **Table/Query**............................... `Alt`+`↓`
   from which to draw value list in **Row Source Type**
   text box if unbound control is a combo box.

9. Select table or query name..................... `Alt`+`↓`
   in **Row Source** text box.

10. Set **Limit to List** text box to Yes.

11. Type macro name.............................. *macro name*
    to run after user input in **After Update** text box.

12. Make other changes to properties as desired.

13. Double–click `▭`........................... `Alt`+`Shift`, `C`
    of property sheet to close.

Change Tab Order

*Changes the default tab order (the order in which they were
added to the form design) of selectable controls.*

1. View form design.

2. Select **Edit**, **Tab Order**................... `Alt`+`E`, `B`

3. Select desired **Section** option.

4. Click selector to left of field name to move.

   OR
   Click and drag selectors of multiple field names to
   move.

5. Drag selected fields to new location.

6. Click `  OK  ` ....`↵`

Auto Tab Order

Automatically sets tab order to start at upper left and proceed from left to right, top to bottom.

1. Select **Edit, Tab Order** .... `Alt`+`E`,`B`

2. Select **Auto Order** .... `A`

3. Click `OK` .... `↵`

Form Sections

Controls how a form appears on the screen and how a form is printed.

Form header	Appears at top of screen and at top of printed page, but not in Datasheet view. May be kept from being printed by setting **Display When** property.
Page header	Appears only at top of printed page.
Detail	Contains controls for records, number of records limited by screen or page size.
Page footer	Appears only at bottom of printed page.
Form footer	Appears at bottom of screen and on last page of printed forms, but not in Datasheet view. May be kept from being printed by setting **Display When** property.

Add/Delete Header and Footer

> *NOTE: Form and page headers and footers are always added as a pair.*

1. View form design.

2. Select **Format** menu .... `Alt`+`O`

3. Select desired header/footer option to add/clear.

Change Section Height

1. Place pointer at bottom edge of section to change.

2. Drag edge to desired new location.

Change Form Width

1. Place pointer at right edge of form.

2. Drag edge to desired new location.

Form and Section Properties

Display Section Property Sheet

> NOTE: The contents of the property sheet varies depending on the section selected.

Double–click section or section header.

OR

1. Place pointer on section or section header and click to select.

2. Click 📝 .... `Alt`+`V`, `I`

Display Form Property Sheet

Double–click gray area to right of any section.

OR

1. Click gray area to right of any section.

2. Click 📝

OR

1. Select **E**dit, Select Fo**r**m .... `Alt`+`E`, `R`

2. Select **V**iew, Proper**t**ies .... `Alt`+`V`, `T`

Change Form or Section Properties

1. Select form or section.

2. Display property sheet.

3. Choose desired property category.

CHANGE FORM OR SECTION PROPERTIES (CONTINUED)

4. Click desired property .... ↓

5. Type desired value .... *value*

   NOTE: Options vary depending on form, section or property chosen.

6. Repeat steps 4–5 for each change.

7. Click 🖼 to close .... Alt + V , I

Set Default View for Form

   NOTE: The default view controls how the form appears when opened.

1. Open form property sheet.

2. Select desired option .... Alt + ↓
   in **Default View** text box.

3. Double–click ▭ .... Alt + Space , C
   of property to close.

Set Default Editing Mode

Controls what mode is available when form is opened.

1. Open form property sheet.

2. Select desired option .... Alt + ↓
   in **Default Editing** text box.

3. Double–click ▭ .... Alt + Space , C
   of property to close.

Change Table or Query

1. Open form property sheet.
2. Select desired table or query .... `Alt`+`↓`
   in **Record Source** text box.
3. Double–click control menu box `Alt`+`Space`, `C`
   in **Default View** text box to close.

Change Underlying Query

1. View form in Design view.
2. Open form property sheet.
3. Click Record source text box.
4. Click `⋯`
5. Make desired changes to query.
6. Close **Query** builder .... `Alt`+`F`, `C`

Create Form Template

Determines default characteristics of any new form to which it is applied.

1. Select **View**, **Options** .... `Alt`+`V`, `O`
2. Select **Category** list .... `Alt`+`C`
3. Choose **Form & Report Design** .... `↓`
4. Select **Items** box .... `Alt`+`I`
5. Type name of Form Template .... *name*
6. Click `OK` .... `↵`

   NOTE: *Settings for form templates are saved in system database (system.mda) not in user database.*

Create Subform

Displays data from another table, or from another record in the same table when placed in another form. See below to place subform on main form.

1. Using directions for creating a form *(see Create Form, page 283)*, create desired subform.

2. Double–click ⬛ to close form.

3. Type name of form .... *name*

4. Click ⬛ **OK** ⬛ .... ⬛

Add Subform to Main Form

1. Open main form in Design view.

2. Make space for addition of subform, if necessary.

3. Click **Database Window** .... ⬛F11⬛
    to switch to Database view.

4. Click ⬛ if necessary.

5. Drag icon for desired subform to desired location on main form.

    NOTE: There must be enough room on main form for subform.

6. Adjust size and location of subform, if desired.

    *NOTE: After adding the subform to the main form, form data should be linked (see **Link Main Form and Subform**, page 284).*

Create Form and Subform Using Wizard

1. Click 🖳 in Database window.

2. Click **New** .... `Alt`+`N`

3. Select desired **Table/Query** .... `Alt`+`↓`

4. Click **Form Wizard** button .... `Alt`+`W`

5. Choose **Main/Subform** .... `↓`

6. Click **OK** .... `↵`

7. Follow directions in **Main/Subform Wizard** dialog boxes.

Change Subform Design from Main Form

1. Double–click subform control in Design view, with subform *not* selected.

2. Change subform design, as desired.

3. Double–click subform ⊟ ...... `Alt`+`Space`, `C` to close.

4. Click **Yes** .... `↵` to save changes.

5. Click edge of subform to select in main form, to display changes.

6. Click inside subform control.

7. Press **Enter** .... `↵`

Switch Between Form and Datasheet Views in Subform

> *NOTE:*   *Use this feature only if **Set Views Allowed** is set to **Both**.*

1. View main form in Form view.
2. Click subform.
3. Select **V**iew, S**u**bform Datasheet ... `Alt`+`V`, `U`

Re-query Subform

Press **Shift+F9** .... `Shift`+`F9`

Link Main Form and Subform

> *NOTE:*   *Access automatically links a main form and a subform if they both are based on tables and the default relationships between the tables are defined (the primary key field and matching field are linked, see **Set Relationship Between Tables,** page 253) or if the main form and subform each has a field with the same name and data type and the field on the main form is the primary key of the underlying table. If these criteria are not met, the tables must be linked manually.*

1. View Form design.
2. Double-click edge of subform to display subform property sheet.
3. Type field name .... *field name* from subform to link to records in master form in **Link Child Fields** text box.
4. Type field name .... *field name* in main form to link to records in subform in **Link Master Fields** text box.
5. Double-click ⬜ to close .... `Alt`+`Space`, `C`

Create Subform Based on Query

Includes, sorts or limits values from several tables, or displays summary data form a crosstab query.

1. Create and save query for subform.

   NOTE: Include field to link subform to main form.

2. Create subform, using query as basis.
3. Add subform to main form.
4. Double–click edge of subform to display subform property sheet.
5. Type field name ....*field name*
   from subform to link to records
   in master form in **Link Child Fields** text box.
6. Type field name ....*field name*
   in master form to link to records
   in subform in **Link Master Fields** text box.
7. Double–click 🗕 to close .... **Alt** + **Shift** , **C**

Create Two Levels of Subform

Typically used for a table with a one–to–many relationship with the table in the first subform, which has a one–to–many relationship with table in second subform.

1. Create first subform and drag onto main form.
2. Create second subform and drag onto main form.
3. Create hidden unbound text box on main form.
4. Display text box property sheet.
5. Click drop–down button to display **All Properties**.
6. Type field name ....*field name*
   that links first subform and second one.

CREATE TWO LEVELS OF SUBFORM (CONTINUED)

7. Click **No** in **Visible** text box .... 【Alt】+【↓】, 【↓】

8. Enter expression that gives same value as linking field on second subform in **Control Source** text box.

    EXAMPLE: [first subform name].Form![linking field name from first subform]

    *NOTE: See **Expressions**, page 322 and **Define Expression**, below.*

9. Click second subform to display its property sheet.

10. Type hidden text box name............................*name* in **Link Master Fields** text box.

11. Type linking field name ....*name* on second subform in **Link Child Fields** text box.

Define Expression

NOTE: An expression can contain any number of arithmetic operators, such as +, −, <, and built−in functions to return the current date, counts, averages and other values.

Enter Expression in Text Box

1. View form in Design view.

2. Create or select text box to contain expression.

3. Click in control text box.

4. Type **equal sign** (=) .... 【=】

5. Type expression.

    NOTE: If a field name or control name used in an expression is more than one word long or contain special characters, enclose it in square brackets: [].

Enter Expression in Property Sheet

Performs a calculation in a control other than a text box, or creates expression with Expression Builder.

1. View form in Design view.
2. Create or select text box to contain expression.
3. Click **Properties** 🖺
4. Click in Control Source property.
5. Type expression.

Name Expression

> NOTE: Expression names may be used in other expressions on the form. The name must be unique among control names on the form, field or control names in the expression, and field names in the underlying query or table.

1. Double–click edge of field containing expression to display property sheet.
2. Type unique name in **Control Name** box .... *name*
3. Double–click ⬛ .... **Alt**+**Space** , **C**

Add Page Numbers

1. View form header or footer in Design view.
2. Click **Text box** [abl]
3. Create text box in header or footer where page number is to appear.
4. Click in text box to create insertion point.
5. Type *=page* in text box .... **=PAGE**

Add Current Date

1. View form in Design View.

2. Create/select text box where date or time is to appear.

3. Click **Properties** 🖼️

4. Type =*date()* .... ▨ⅅ𝔸𝕋𝔼 ( )
   in **Default Value** box.

5. Double–click ▭ .... ꓮ𝗅𝗍 + 𝖲𝗉𝖺𝖼𝖾 , ꓚ

Combine Text Values

1. View form in Design view.

2. Create/select text box where combined text is to appear.

3. Click text box to create insertion point.

4. Type **equal sign** (=) in text box...................... ▤

5. Type first text field name .... ▨*name* ❩
   enclosed in brackets.

   OR

   Type text enclosed in quotations ..... ▨*name* ▨

6. Type **ampersand** (&) .... ▨

7. Repeat steps 4–5 for each additional field or bit of text to add, ending with a right bracket or quotation mark.

   EXAMPLE: =[last name]&","&[first name].

Set Layout Property for Print or Screen

*NOTE: The **Layout for Print** property determines whether the fonts used in a form are screen fonts or printer fonts. Printer fonts correspond to the printer currently selected in printer setup.*

1. Double–click gray area outside form to display form property sheet.

    OR

    Click gray area outside form.......... `Alt`+`V`, `I`

2. Click **Layout for Print** text box.

3. Reveal drop–down list.............................. `Alt`+`↓`

4. Click `Yes` to use printer fonts.

    OR

    Click `No` to use screen fonts.

5. Double–click `▄` to close .... `Alt`+`Space`, `C`

ENTER/EDIT DATA

NOTE: Access automatically saves new records.

—IN FORM VIEW—

1. Click `▶|`, `▶` .... `Alt`+`R`, `D`

2. Type desired value in first field..................... *value*.

3. Press **Tab** .... `Tab`

4. Repeat steps 2–3 until complete.

5. Click `▶` to move to next blank record.

ENTER/EDIT DATA (CONTINUED)

6. Repeat for each additional record to add.

7. Double–click ⬛ to close form when finished.

—IN DATASHEET VIEW—

1. Place insertion point in last blank record......... ⬛

   NOTE: The blank record appears with an asterisk in the left margin.

   To view only newly added records:

   Select **R**ecords, **D**ata Entry............. `Alt`+`R`,`D`

2. Type desired value in first field .... *value*

3. Press **Tab** .... `Tab`

4. Repeat steps 2–3 until complete.

5. Move to next blank record .... `Tab`

6. Repeat for each additional record to add.

7. Double–click ⬛ to close datasheet when finished.

Access All Records

Select **R**ecords, **S**how All Records .... `Alt`+`R`,`S`

Replace Data in Field

   NOTE: Access automatically saves changes to fields when you move to the next record. A pencil icon appears at left of record in Datasheet view and at the top left of the window in Form view to indicate that the changes have not yet been saved.

1. Place insertion point in field to change .... `Tab`

2. Type desired new value................................. *value*

Add Data to Field

> *NOTE:* *Access automatically saves changes to fields when you move to the next record. A pencil icon appears at left of record in Datasheet view and at the top left of the window in Form view to indicate that the changes have not yet been saved.*

1. Place insertion point in field to change........... `Tab`

2. Place insertion point at desired position........... `F2`

3. Type data to add... *data*

Cancel Changes to Field Data

Press **Esc** while still in field................................. `Esc`

Cancel Changes to Record Data

Press **Esc** twice while still in record............ `Esc`, `Esc`

Enter, Edit and Select Data
Navigate

MOVE TO:	PRESS/CLICK:
Next field or next record	`Tab` or `↓`
Previous field or record	`Shift`+`Tab` or `↑`
First field	`Home`
Last field	`End`
Next record, Form view	`▶` or `Ctrl`+`Page Down`
Previous record, Form view	`◀` or `Ctrl`+`Page Up`

NAVIGATE (CONTINUED)

MOVE TO:	PRESS/CLICK:
Next record, Datasheet view	↓
Previous record, Datasheet view	↑
First record, Form view	⏮
First record, first field	Ctrl + Home
Last record, Form view	⏭
Last record, last field	Ctrl + End
Scroll up one page	Page Up
Scroll down one page	Page Down
Next form section	F6
Next field of main form, from subform	Ctrl + Tab
First field of main form from subform.	Ctrl + Shift + Home
Open combo box, Form view	Alt + ↓
Open Zoom box	Shift + F2

Edit

TO:	PRESS:
Insert line return in field	Ctrl + ↵
Duplicate field value from previous record.	Ctrl + "
Revert to default value	Ctrl + Alt + Space
Save changes	Shift + ↵
Re–query records	Shift + F9

Select Data

TO: **PRESS:**

Select or remove select from field .... `F2`

Extend selection in field .... `Shift`+`↑` `↓` `←` `→`

Select additional adjacent .... `Shift`+`↑` `↓` `←` `→`
datasheet fields.

Select current datasheet column........... `Ctrl`+`Space`

Select current datasheet record .... `Shift`+`Space`

Select multiple .... `Shift`+`Space`, `Shift`+`↑` `↓`
datasheet records.

Select entire form field............................ *click field label*

Select entire datasheet field .... *click left field edge*

Select datasheet column.................... *click field selector*

Select datasheet record .... *click record selector*

Select all datasheet records ..... *click datasheet selector*

> *NOTE:* *The datasheet selector is located to the left of field selectors, above record selectors.*

Format Datasheet

> *NOTE:* *Changes made to a datasheet for a form or table must be saved manually to be permanent. Changes made to a datasheet for a query cannot be saved.*

Change Row Height

1. Place pointer between two record selectors.
2. Click and drag to desired width.

OR

1. Select **Format**, **Row Height**............ `Alt`+`O`,`R`
2. Type new height .... *number*
3. Click [**OK**] .... `↵`

Change Column Width

1. Display Datasheet view.

2. Place pointer at right edge of desired field selector.

3. Click and drag border to desired size.

Move Column

1. Click field selector for desired column.

2. Click and drag field selector to new location.

Hide Column

1. Place pointer at right edge of field selector for column to hide.

2. Click and drag right border to meet left border.

Show Hidden Column

1. Select **F**ormat, **S**how Columns .... `Alt`+`O`, `S`

2. Select column(s) to show .... `↓`

3. Select **S**how .... `Alt`+`S`

4. Click `Close` .... `Alt`+`C`

Freeze Columns in Screen Position

1. Click field selector for column(s) to freeze.

2. Select **F**ormat, Free**z**e Columns ..... `Alt`+`O`, `Z`

Unfreeze Columns

Select **F**ormat, **U**nfreeze All Columns .. `Alt`+`O`, `U`

Change Font

1. Select F**o**rmat, **F**ont...................... Alt + O , F
2. Select desired font.. ↓
3. Select Font St**y**le .... Alt + Y , ↓
4. Select Font **S**ize .... Alt + S , ↓
5. Click OK .... ↵

Copy/Move Records
Copy Records from One Datasheet to Another

> *NOTE:* *Data from copied records is pasted in*
> *original column order, regardless of field*
> *names in datasheet. Columns in datasheet*
> *to receive pasted data should be arranged*
> *in correct order and have matching data*
> *types as well as compatible properties.*
> *Data may also be copied from other*
> *applications.*

1. Select records to copy.

2. Press **Ctrl+C** .... Ctrl + C

3. View datasheet to receive copy.

4. Select records .... Ctrl + V
   to replace and press **Ctrl+V**.

   To append copy to end of datasheet:

   Select **E**dit, Paste Appen**d**.............. Alt + E , D

Cut and Paste Records from One
Datasheet to Another

NOTE: *Data from cut records is pasted in original*
column order, regardless of field names in
datasheet. Columns in datasheet to receive
pasted data should be arranged in correct
order and have matching data types as well
as compatible properties. Data may also
be cut from other applications.

1. Select records to cut.

2. Press **Ctrl+X** .... Ctrl + X

3. Click ⸢   OK   ⸥ .... ↵

4. View datasheet to receive data.

5. Select records .... Ctrl + V
   to replace and press **Ctrl+V**.

To append cut records to end of datasheet:

Select **E̲dit, Paste Appen̲d** .... Alt + E , D

Copy Records to Form

NOTE: *Data from copied records is pasted in*
fields with matching names. If no match is
found for a field, that data is not pasted.

1. Select records to copy.

2. Press **Ctrl+C** .... Ctrl + C

3. View form to receive copy.

4. Select records .... Ctrl + V
   to replace and press **Ctrl+V**.

To append copy to end of datasheet:

Select **E̲dit, Paste Appen̲d** .... Alt + E , D

Cut and Paste Records to Form

> NOTE: Data from cut records is pasted in fields with matching names. If no match is found for a field, that data is not pasted.

1. Select records to cut.

2. Press **Ctrl+X** .... `Ctrl`+`X`

3. View datasheet to receive data.

   To replace selected records:
   a. Select records to replace.

   b. Press **Ctrl+V** .... `Ctrl`+`V`

   To append cut records to form:
   Select **Edit**, **Paste Append** menu.... `Alt`+`E`,`D`

Undo Changes

   To undo all changes to current field or record:
   Select **Edit**, **Undo Current Field** ..... `Alt`+`E`,`N`

   To undo most recent changes to field or record:
   Select **Edit**, **Undo Typing** .... `Alt`+`E`,`U`

   To undo changes to saved record:
   Select **Edit**, **Undo Saved Record** .... `Alt`+`E`,`U`

298 ACCESS

FIND AND SORT DATA

Find Matching Field Data

1. Click field selector or any field in column.
2. Click **Find** 🔍 .... `Alt`+`E`, `F`
3. Type value................................... `Alt`+`N`
   to match in **Find What** text box.
4. Select **Find Next** or **Find First**, as desired.
5. Repeat step 4 for each additional record to find.

Repeat Search after Closing Find Dialog Box

Press **Shift+F4** .... `Shift`+`F4`

Find Records Using Find Options

1. Click field to match or, in Datasheet view, click field selector or any field in column.
2. Click 🔍 .... `Alt`+`E`, `F`
3. Type value in **Find What** text box .... *value*.
4. Select part of field................... `Alt`+`H`, `Alt`+`↓`
   to match in **Where** list.
5. Select **Current Field** or **All Fields** search range..
6. Select **Up** or **Down**, as desired.
7. Click **Match Case** if desired .... `Alt`+`C`
8. Click **Search Fields as Formatted** .... `Alt`+`F`
   if desired.
   NOTE: Matches formatting of number, date, currency, and yes/no fields, rather than data actually stored in table.
9. Select **Find Next** or **Find First**, as desired.

Find and Replace Data

1. Click field to match or, in Datasheet view, click field selector or any field in column.

2. Select **Edit**, **Replace**...................... `Alt`+`E`,`R`

3. Type data to replace in **Find What** text box .... *data*.

4. Type replacement data .... `Alt`+`P`
   in **Replace With** text box.

5. Select **Current Field** or **All Fields** search range, as desired.

6. Click **Match Case** to restrict search........ `Alt`+`C`

7. Click **Match Whole Field**...................... `Alt`+`W`
   to restrict search.

   To replace text in next matching field only:
   Click `Replace` .... `Alt`+`R`

   To replace text in all matching fields at once:
   Click `Replace All` .... `Alt`+`A`

   To view next matching field only:
   Click `Find Next` .... `Alt`+`N`

8. Click **Close** when finished .... `Esc`

9. Click `OK` to confirm changes.......... `↵`

Filter and Sort Records

Sorts and displays specified records in Form or Datasheet view. Filters are similar to queries, but are not usually saved with the form.

1. View desired form or datasheet.

2. Click **Edit Filter/Sort** .... Alt + R , F

3. Drag desired field from field list to **Field** cell in lower part of window.

4. Click **Sort** to choose sort order .... Alt + ↓

5. Place pointer in **Criteria** cell ....*criteria* and type search criteria.

6. Repeat steps 3–5 for each additional field to search or sort.

7. Click **Apply Filter/Sort** .... Alt + R , Y

Show All Records

Removes a filter.

Click **Show All Records** .... Alt + R , S

Sort Records Quickly

1. Select field by which to sort in Form view.
   OR
   Select column(s) by which to sort in Datasheet view.

2. Click desired sort order
   OR
   a. Select **Records, Quick Sort** ...... Alt + R , D
   b. Select **Ascending** or **Descending** ...... A / D

Save Filter as Query

> NOTE: When a form or datasheet is closed, the filter is not saved unless it is saved as a query.

1. View filter to save.

2. Select **File**, **Save As Query**............. `Alt`+`F`, `A`

3. Type query name................................. *query name*

4. Click `OK` .... `↵`

Use Query as Filter

> NOTE: A query can be used as a filter if (a) it is a select query not containing totals, (b) it is based on the same table or underlying query and(c) it does not include any other table or query as the form or datasheet viewed.

1. Click **Edit Filter/Sort** .... `Alt`+`R`, `F`

2. Select **File**, **Load From Query** .... `Alt`+`F`, `L`

3. Choose query name from list box .... `↓`

4. Click `OK` .... `↵`

5. Click **Apply Filter/Sort** .... `Alt`+`R`, `Y`

REPORTS

Create New Report Using Report Wizards

1. Click 〔▦ Report〕 in Database window... ⌗Alt⌗+⌗V⌗, ⌗R⌗

2. Click 〔 **New** 〕.............................. ⌗Alt⌗+⌗N⌗

3. Click drop–down arrow......................... ⌗Alt⌗+⌗↓⌗
   to select table or query.

4. Click **Report Wizards** 〔▦〕............... ⌗Alt⌗+⌗W⌗

5. Select desired report style .... ⌗↓⌗

6. Click 〔 **OK** 〕.............................. ⌗↵⌗

7. Follow screen instructions for specific form type.

Create Report

1. Click 〔▦ Report〕 in Database window.... ⌗Alt⌗+⌗V⌗, ⌗R⌗

2. Click 〔 **New** 〕.............................. ⌗Alt⌗+⌗N⌗

3. Select table or query............................. ⌗↓⌗

4. Click **Blank Report**............................ ⌗Alt⌗+⌗B⌗

Open Report

1. View Database window.

2. Click 〔▦ Report〕 .... ⌗Alt⌗+⌗V⌗, ⌗R⌗

3. Select report .... ⌗↓⌗

OPEN REPORT (CONTINUED)

4. Click **D**esign .... `Alt`+`D`
   to view report in Design view.
   OR

   Click **P**review .... `Alt`+`P`
   to view report as it will appear when printed.

Save Report

1. Select **F**ile menu in Report window ...... `Alt`+`F`

2. Select **S**ave .... `S`

3. Type name..*report name*
   in text box, if saving for first time.

4. Click [**OK**] .... `↵`

Close Report

Select **F**ile, **C**lose .... `Alt`+`F`,`C`

Preview Report

> *NOTE:* *Sample Preview displays font, font size*
> *and layout features with a few records,*
> *while Print Preview displays the report*
> *exactly as it will be printed. Both are close*
> *up views.*

Sample Preview

1. View report in Design view.

2. Click **Sample Preview** 🔍 .... `Alt`+`F`, `M`

Print Preview

1. View report in Design view.

2. Click **Print Preview** 🔲 .... `Alt`+`F`, `V`

3. View Database window.

4. Click 🔲 .... `Alt`+`V`, `R`

5. Select report to preview.............................. `↓`

6. Click ⌊Preview⌋ .... `Alt`+`P`

Return to Database Window

Returns to Database window from Sample Preview or Print Preview.

Click 🔲 .... `Alt`+`F`, `C`

Page Through Report

1. View report in Sample Preview or Print Preview.

2. Click desired navigation button.

    OR

    a. Double–click **Page Number** text box, near navigation buttons.

    b. Enter desired page number .... *number*

    c. Press **Enter** .... `↵`

View Entire Page

1. View report in Sample Preview or Print Preview.

2. Click 🔲 .... `Z`

Print Report

1. View report in Design view, Sample Preview or Print Preview.
   OR
   Select report in Database window.

2. Click 🖨 if available...................... `Alt`+`F`, `P`
3. Select desired **Print Range** option.
4. Click drop–down arrow .... `Alt`+`Q`, `Alt`+`↓`
   to change **Print Quality**.

5. Type number in **Copies** box if desired.... `Alt`+`C`
6. Set other options, as desired.
7. Click [**OK**] .... `↵`

Save Report to File

> *NOTE: A report saved to a file may be printed at any later time.*

1. View report in **Design**, **Sample Preview** or **Print Preview**.
   OR
   Select report in Database window.

2. Click [Report] if available .... `Alt`+`F`, `P`
3. Click **Print to File** to select.................. `Alt`+`L`
4. Set other options, as desired.
5. Click [**OK**] .... `↵`
6. Type filename .... *name*
7. Click [**OK**] .... `↵`

Print Report Definition

Includes report's fields, controls and control properties. Used to reconstruct a report.

1. View Database window.

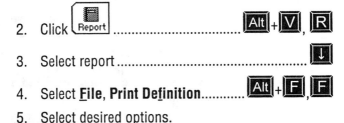

2. Click [Report] .... `Alt`+`V`, `R`

3. Select report .... `↓`

4. Select **File**, **Print De_f_inition**............ `Alt`+`F`, `F`

5. Select desired options.

6. Click [OK   ] .... `↵`

Create Bound Text Box

Creates text boxes used to contain data. Unbound text boxes contain other text or design elements.

1. View report in Design view.

2. Click **Field List** 🖽 .... `Alt`+`V`, `L`

3. Click Field List window; select desired field ..... `↓`

   OR

   Double–click list title bar to select all fields.

4. Click and drag fields to desired report section. Place upper left corner of pointer at desired location of upper left corner of top field. Release mouse button.

Create Unbound Controls

Creates controls used for labels, graphic elements and other elements on a report that are not used to display data.

1. View report in Design view.

ACCESS

CREATE UNBOUND CONTROLS (CONTINUED)

2. Click tool for desired unbound control to create in the tool box.
3. Place pointer (its appearance will reflect the tool in use) on report at desired upper left corner of control location.
4. Click to create default sized control.
   OR
   Click and drag to desired size.

Create Bound Control
Creates formatted controls to contain data from the database.
1. Click tool for desired control to create.
2. Click **Field List** ▦ .... `Alt`+`V`, `L`
3. Select desired field .... `↓`
4. Click and drag field to desired location of upper left corner of control.
5. Click to create default sized control.

Create Calculated Text Box
Creates control to contain expressions and functions. For example, a calculated text box may be used to display the current date, time, page number, calculations based on field values, or concatenations of text fields. (See Expressions, page 322.)

1. Click `ab|` in the tool box.
2. Place pointer at desired upper left corner of text box.
3. Click to place default sized text box.
   OR
   Click and drag to text box to desired size.
4. Place pointer inside text box and click.
5. Type **equal sign** (=).. `≡`
6. Type expression.

Move Control

1. Select control or controls to move.
2. Place pointer on control border to move control and attached label.
   OR
   Place pointer on upper left corner to move label or control only.
3. Click and drag to new location.
   NOTE: A label or control alone cannot be dragged to a different report section.

Control Shape of Label

1. Click label.
2. Type first line of text to desired length............. *text*
3. Press **Ctrl+Enter** .... `Ctrl` + `↵`

Remaining lines wrap to match first line length.

Change Control Properties
Display Property Sheet

NOTE: The contents of the property sheet will vary depending on the control type selected.

Double–click control.

Change Control Properties

1. Select control.
2. Display property sheet *(see above)*.
3. Click drop–down arrow to select desired property category.
   NOTE: Properties vary depending on type of control selected.
4. Click desired property text box .... `↓`
5. Type desired value .... `Alt` + `↓`
6. Repeat steps 4–5 for each property change.
7. Click 🖾 to close .... `Alt` + `V` , `I`

Set Data Format

1. Select control.

2. Display property sheet.

3. Click drop–down arrow to choose **Data Properties** category.

4. Click **Format** text box.

5. Click drop–down arrow .... `Alt`+`↓`

6. Select desired format.

7. Click **Properties** 📇 to close .. `Alt`+`Space`, `C`

Set Report to Hide Duplicates

Stops a text box containing the same value as the text box in the previous record from being printed.

1. Select control.

2. Display property sheet.

3. Click drop–down button to choose **Layout Properties**.

4. Click **Hide Duplicates** text box.

5. Click drop–down arrow .... `Alt`+`↓`

6. Click **Yes** .... `↓`

7. Click **Properties** 📇 to close .. `Alt`+`Space`, `C`

Create Check Boxes, Option Buttons and Option Groups

> NOTE: The technique for displaying data in various forms is the same in both reports and forms.

Add Page Break

1. Click ⊞ on tool box.

2. Click report at desired location of beginning of new page.

   NOTE: Avoid placing a page break where it would split a control.

Add Report or Page Header and Footer

NOTE: Report and page headers and footers are always added as a pair.

1. Select **Format** menu .... `Alt`+`O`

2. Select **Report Header/Footer** or **Page Header/Footer**, as desired.

Delete Report or Page Header and Footer

1. Select **Format** menu .... `Alt`+`O`

2. Select desired header/footer option to delete.

Change Section Height

1. Place pointer at bottom edge of section to change.

2. Click and drag edge to desired new location.

Report and Section Properties

Display Section Property Sheet

NOTE: The contents of the property sheet varies depending on the section selected.

1. Place pointer on section or section header and click to select.

2. Click **Properties** 📇 .... `Alt`+`V`, `I`

ACCESS   311

Display Report Property Sheet

Double–click gray area to right of any section.

OR

1. Select **E**dit, Select **R**eport.............. Alt + E , R
2. Select **V**iew, Propert**i**es .... Alt + V , I

Change Report or Section Properties

1. Select report or section.
2. Display property sheet.
3. Click desired property.
4. Type desired value.

   NOTE: Options vary depending on report, section or property chosen.

5. Repeat steps 3–4 for each change.
6. Click **Properties** 🖼 to close .. Alt + Space , C

Create Report Template

   NOTE: A report template is used to determine default characteristics of any new report to which it is applied.

1. Select **V**iew, **O**ptions .... Alt + V , O
2. Select **C**ategory list .... Alt + C
3. Choose **Form & Report Design**..................... ↓
4. Select **I**tems box .... Alt + I
5. Type name of **Report Template**. .....*template name*
6. Click ⟨ **OK** ⟩ .... ↵

   NOTE: Settings for report template are saved in system database (system.mda), not in user database.

Sort Data in Report

Sorts by up to ten fields or expressions. The same field or expression may be used more than once.

1. View report in Design view.

2. Click ⌸ .... `Alt`+`V`, `S`

3. Click drop–down arrow .... `Alt`+`↓`
   to select first field to sort by.

4. Select first text box of **Sort Order** column ...... `Tab`

5. Select sort order .... `Alt`+`↓`

6. Select **Next Field/Expression** text box............ `Tab`

7. Repeat steps 3–6 for each field or expression by which to sort.

Group Report Data

Groups data when sorted, and displays it in sections in the report. The section may be empty, or may contain controls that appear only at the beginning (head) or end (foot) of the group. Up to ten layers of groups may be chosen.

1. View report in Design view.

2. Click ⌸ .... `Alt`+`V`, `S`

3. Set sort order.

4. Select desired field in **Field/Expression** column to group on.

5. Click **Group Header** text box............................ `F6`
   in Group Properties area.

GROUP REPORT DATA (CONTINUED)

6. Click drop–down arrow .... `Alt`+`↓`
   and choose desired option.

7. Click **Group Footer** text box............................ `↓`

8. Click drop–down arrow .... `Alt`+`↓`
   and choose desired option.

9. Repeat steps 4–8 for each field to group on.

10. Double–click `▬` to close .... `Alt`+`Space` , `C`

11. Add desired controls to new group header or group
    footer sections.

Set Grouping Range and Interval

*Uses the Group On and Group Interval properties to determine
the value or range of values that will begin a new group. Each
data type has different options related to the type in the **Group
On** text box. Text fields may be grouped based on first few
letters, date fields based on time periods, etc.*

1. Select desired field or expression to set grouping
   range and interval in **Sorting and Grouping** box.

2. Click **Group On** in **Group Properties**........ `F6` , `↓`

3. Click drop–down arrow .... `Alt`+`↓`
   to select desired range.

   *NOTE: If **Group On** is set to **Each Value**, then
   each different value will form a group.*

4. Click **Group Interval** text box .... `Tab`

5. Type desired interval.

   *NOTE: For example, for a date field, if **Group On**
   text box is set to month and group interval
   is set to six, groups would be set into six–
   month periods. For a text field, this
   indicates how many of the prefix letters to
   use to group on.*

Change Sorting and Grouping Order

1. Click selector to left of field or expression to move in **Sorting and Grouping** dialog box.
2. Click and drag selector to new location.

Keep Groups Together

1. Click field or expression to group on in **Sorting and Grouping** dialog box.
2. Select desired .... `F6`, `↓`, `Alt`+`↓`
   Keep Together option in **Group Properties** section.

Add Sorting/Grouping Field or Expression

1. Click selector to left of desired field or expression in **Sorting and Grouping** dialog box.
2. Press **Insert** .... `Ins`
3. Select field or type expression on which to sort or group in new, blank row.

Delete Sorting or Grouping Field or Expression

1. Click selector to left of field or expression to delete in **Sorting and Grouping** dialog box.
2. Press **Delete** .... `Del`

Add Subreport to Main Report

Combines a main report with related, parallel or unrelated subreports. Main reports and subreports may also contain up to two nested subforms.

1. Design and save subreport(s).
2. View main report in Design view.
3. Switch to Database window .... `F11`
4. Drag desired subreport to desired section of main report.
5. Move and size subreport, if necessary.
   NOTE: To link main report and subreport, see below.

Change Subreport Design

1. Double–click subreport with subreport *not* selected.

2. Make desired changes when subreport Design view appears.

3. Double–click subreport ⊟ to close and save.

Link Main Report and Subreport

Displays correct data when a subreport contains data related to the main report. The linking fields need not appear in the report, only in the underlying tables or queries, but the fields must have compatible data and field sizes. Access may automatically link the main report and subreport if they are bound to tables with a set default relationship, or if the primary key of the main table matches a field in the subreport's table or query. To use a calculated value as a subreport link, define a calculated field in the query underlying the subreport.

1. Select subreport in Design view of main report.

2. Click **Properties** 🖺 .... Alt + V , I

3. Click **Link Child Fields** text box .... ↓

4. Type name of linking field in subreport ..*field name*

5. Click **Link Master Fields** text box .... ↓

6. Type name of linking field ....*field name* in main report.

7. Double–click **Properties** list .... Alt + Space , C in control menu box to close.

316   ACCESS

Define Expression for Report

NOTE: An expression in a text box on a report is not stored in the database, but calculated each time the report is displayed or printed.

Enter Expression in Text Box

1. View report in Design view.
2. Select text box to contain expression.
   OR
   a. Click **Text Box** ⌨abl in tool box.
   b. Click form at desired location of default sized text box.
3. Click inside text box.
4. Press **equal sign** (=) .... ▣
5. Type desired expression .... *expression*

Enter Expression in Property Sheet

1. View report in Design view.
2. Select text box to contain expression.
   OR
   a. Click **Text Box** ⌨abl in tool box.
   b. Click form at desired location of default sized text box.
3. Click **Properties** ▤ .... Alt+V, I
4. Place insertion point in **Control Source** text box in **Data Properties Category**.
5. Type **equal sign** (=) .... ▣
6. Click ▭ .... *expression*
7. Press **Shift+F2** .... Shift+F2
   to see expression in larger box.

Add Current Date or Page Numbering

1. View report in Design view.
2. Click **Text Box** 🔲abl🔲 in tool box.
3. Click report at desired location.
   NOTE: Page numbers are usually placed in a report's header or footer sections.
4. Click inside text box.
5. Type **equal sign** (=)................................🔳**=**
6. Type *date*.................................🔳**D**🔳**A**🔳**T**🔳**E**
   to include current date.
   OR

   Type *page*.................................🔳**P**🔳**A**🔳**G**🔳**E**
   to include page numbering.
   *NOTE: To add page numbers or dates in other formats using the Expression Builder, see **Expressions,** page 322.*

Combine Text Values

1. View report in Design view.
2. Create/select text box where combined text is to appear.
3. Type **equal sign** (=)in text box ....🔳**=**
4. Type name of first text field................*[field name]* enclosed in brackets.
5. Type **ampersand (&)**................................🔳**&**
6. Repeat steps 4–5 for each additional field or bit of text to add, ending with a right bracket or quotation mark.
   EXAMPLE: =[last name]&", "&[first name]

MACROS

Create Macro

1. Click ⊞ Macro in Database window.

2. Click **New** .... Alt + N

Assign Action to Macro

1. Click first text box in **Action** column in Macro window.

2. Click drop–down arrow .... Alt + ↓
   and select desired action.

   OR

   a. Press **F11** to view Database window F11

   b. Drag desired form, report, query or table to open or macro to run to text box in Macro window.

3. Click adjacent text box in **Comments** column. Tab

4. Type comment if desired .... *comment*

5. Move to **Action** arguments section F6

6. Type desired arguments.

Move Action

1. Click selector button to left of desired action to move in Macro window.

2. Click and drag action to new location.

Delete Action

1. Click selector button to left of desired action to move in Macro window.

2. Press **Delete** .... `Del`

Set Macro Arguments

Gives Access information on how to carry out macro actions. Usually, expressions can be used (see below for exceptions, see also Expressions, page 322). When actions are added to a macro by dragging, Access automatically sets an argument for it.

1. Create macro.

2. Move to Action Arguments .... `F6` section of window.

3. Click drop–down arrow .... `Alt`+`↓` and make selection to complete each text box as desired.

   OR

   Type **Equal Sign** (=) .... `=` followed by expression.

   NOTE: It is best to complete the arguments in top to bottom order.

Save Macro

1. Select **File** menu in Macro window .... `Alt`+`F`

2. Select **Save** .... `S`

3. Type macro name............................ *macro name* if saving for the first time.

4. Click `  OK  ` .... `↵`

Run Macro

Click **Run** ⊡ on toolbar of Macro window. [Alt]+[M],[R]

OR

1. Click Macro [Macro] in Database window.
2. Select desired macro name .... [↓]
3. Click [__Run__] .... [Alt]+[R]

Create Macro Group

Contains any number of separate macros in one document and is used to organze macros. All the macros in the group and their steps appear in the group window.

1. Create an empty macro.
2. Click **Macros Names** [xyz] .... [Alt]+[V],[M]
3. Type a macro name in the text box of Macro Name column of each action or set of actions.

   NOTE: For macros of more than one step, the name should be typed to the left of the first step.

4. Create macros, assign actions and set arguments as desired.

Run Macro in Macro Group

Type macro group name, a period, and the macro name where necessary.

Use Control Name in Macro Expression

1. Choose desired source.
2. Press Exclamation Point key (!).......... ......

Access

USE CONTROL NAME IN MACRO EXPRESSION (CONTINUED)

3. Type source name .... 🔲*source name* 🔲
   enclosing it in square brackets if it has any blank
   spaces in it.

4. Type control name .... 🔲*control name* 🔲
   enclosing it in square brackets if it has any blank
   spaces in it.

5. Press Exclamation Point key (!) .... 🔲

   EXAMPLE: Reports![special printout]!volumune!

Add Condition to Macro

1. Click **Conditions** 🔲 .... Alt + V , C
   in Macro window.

2. Place insertion point .... ↓
   in desired action's Condition column.

3. Type conditional expression .... *expression*

4. Enter desired action in action column . Tab , *action*

5. Place insertion point in next action's Condition
   column to enter more actions to take place if same
   condition is satisfied.

6. Type ellipsis .... 🔲🔲🔲

7. Repeat steps 4–6 for each additional step to add.

Debug Macro

1. Open macro.
2. Click **Single Step** ⌨ .... Alt + M , S
3. Run macro *(see Run Macro, page 320).*
4. Click **Step** button for each step to run .... ↵

Open Macro

1. Click ⊞Macro in Database window.
2. Click macro to open .... ↓ , Alt + D

Set Macro to Respond to Event

1. Click **Properties** ⊞ .... Alt + V , I
   in Design View of form.
2. Click desired control, or form itself.
3. Click desired property for event .... ↓
4. Select desired macro from list .... Alt + ↓

EXPRESSIONS

> *NOTE: Expressions are used in forms, reports, macros, queries, and set criteria, perform calculations, and to control printed appearance of data.*

Enter Expression

1. Click desired text box.
2. Type **equal sign** (=) .... =
3. Type expression...................................*expression*
4. Press **Shift+F2**.................................. Shift + F2
   to open **Zoom** box if text box
   is too small to see entire expression.

Use Expression Builder

Helps create expressions for property sheets, criteria cells, and other places in Access where expressions are used.

1. Place insertion point in text box to contain expression.
2. Click ▦

     —IN EXPRESSION BOX—

3. Type desired expression elements.
   OR
   Paste elements from buttons and functions below.

Parts of Expression

ELEMENT:	DEFINITION:
Operator	Operation to perform.
Identifier	Value of field, control or property.
Function	Calculates a value.
Literal	A number, text string, or date used as written.
Constant	An unchanging value.

Use Object Name

    NOTE: An object name refers to a table, form, query, report, control or field.

1. Type **left bracket** ([) .... 🔲
2. Type object name .... *object name*
3. Type **right bracket** (]) .... 🔲

Use Date or Time Value in Expression

1. Type **number symbol** (#) .... 🔲
2. Type date or time in any common format.
3. Type **number symbol** (#) .... 🔲

Use Text in Expressions

1. Type **quotation mark ("")** .... 🔲

2. Type text .... *text*

3. Type **quotation mark ("")** .... 🔲

   NOTE: *If the text string does not contain any spaces, the quotation marks are not necessary.*

Operators Used in Expressions

*	Multiply
+	Add
–	Subtract or negate
/	Divide
\\	Divide integers
^	Raise to the power of exponent
Mod	Divide and return remainder
<	Less than
>	Greater than
<=	Less than or equal
>=	Greater than or equal
=	Equal
<>	Not equal
&	Concatenate (combine) strings
And	Logical and
Eqv	Logical equivalence
Imp	Logical implication
Not	Logical not
Or	Inclusive or
Xor	Exclusive or
Between	Within a range
In	Equal to any of the values in a list
Is	Used with Null or not Null (no value or value)
Like	Compare two strings using wildcard characters

Identifiers Used in Expressions

SYMBOL: FUNCTION:
!   Is followed by the name of a form, report, control or
          field: Forms![EntryForm]![Last name]
.   Is followed by a property name: Forms![Entry
          Form]![Last name].Locked

Functions Used in Expressions

FUNCTION: RETURN:

FUNCTION	RETURN
DAvg	Average of a set of values in domain.
DCount	Number of selected records in domain.
DFirst	Field value from first record in domain.
DLast	Field value from last record in domain.
DLookup	Field value in a domain.
DMin	Minimum of a set of values in domain.
DMax	Maximum of a set of values in domain.
DStDev	Estimate of standard deviation in domain.
DStDevP	Estimate of the standard deviation for sample in domain.
DSum	Sum of a set of values in domain.
DVar	Estimate of variance in domain.
DVarP	Estimate of variance for sample in domain.
Avg	Average of a set of values.
Count	Number of selected records.
First	Field value from first record.
Last	Field value from last record.
Min	Minimum of a set of values.
Max	Maximum of a set of values.
StDev	Estimate of standard deviation.
StDevP	Estimate of standard deviation of sample.
Sum	Sum of set of values.
Var	Variance of set of values.
VarP	Variance of sample set of values.
Choose	Choose value from list of arguments.
Date	Current system date.
DateAdd	Date to which a specified time interval is added.
DateDiff	Time interval between two dates.
DatePart	Specified part of date.

FUNCTIONS USED IN EXPRESSIONS (CONTINUED)

FUNCTION: RETURN:

Day	Day of the month.
Format	Formatted number, date, time, string.
IIf	One of two arguments depending on result of expression.
IsNull	Indication of whether or not expression contains Null value.
Left	Specified number of characters at left of string.
Right	Specified number of characters at right of string.

Index 327

Index

330   Index

W
O
R
D

EXCEL INDEX

A

B

C

Index

331

EXCEL

E
X
C
E
L

Index

Index

POWERPOINT INDEX

Index

337

338

Index

Index 339

POWERPOINT

ACCESS INDEX

Index

341

**A
C
C
E
S
S**

**A
C
C
E
S
S**

Index

344

Index

Index

345

FREE CATALOG
&
UPDATED LISTING

We don't just have books that find your answers faster; we also have books that teach you how to use your computer without the fairy tales and the gobbledygook.

We also have books to improve your typing, spelling and punctuation.

Tear out the slip below and return it to us for a free catalog and mailing list update.

RETURN TODAY!

14 E. 38th St. New York, NY 10016

❏ Please send me your catalog and put me on your mailing list.

_____
Name

_____
Firm (if any)

_____
Address

_____
City, State, Zip